Before the Horror

Before the Horror

THE POPULATION OF HAWAI'I
ON THE EVE OF WESTERN CONTACT

David E. Stannard

Social Science Research Institute
University of Hawaii

Copyright © 1989 by the Social Science Research Institute
University of Hawaii
All rights reserved
Manufactured in the United States of America

ISBN 0-8248-1232-8

Design and manufacture of this book
was handled through Production Services
University of Hawaii Press

Library of Congress Cataloging-in-Publication Data
Stannard, David E.
  Before the horror : the population of Hawai'i on the eve of Western contact / David E. Stannard.
      p.   cm.
  Bibliography: p.
  Includes index.
  ISBN 0-8248-1232-8 : $10.95
    1. Hawaiians—Population. 2. Hawaii—Population—History.
  I. Title.
  GN875.H3S73   1989   88-32127
  304.6'09969—dc19   CIP

∞™ The paper used in this publication meets the minimum requirements of American National Standard for Information Sciences—Permanence of Paper for Printed Library Materials
ANSI Z39.48-1984

Distributed by
University of Hawaii Press
Order Department
2840 Kolowalu Street
Honolulu, Hawaii 96822

*In memory of my father, who,
in the hardest of times,
taught me so much by his courageous,
compassionate, tenacious example.*

For my sons, that they too may learn.

*And for the Hawaiian people,
that they may overcome.*

The injury these people receiv'd from us by communicating this certain destroyer of mankind [syphilis] is not to be repair'd by any method whatever. . . . The man who has rob'd, murder'd and been guilty of all the Catalogue of human crimes is innocent when compar'd to the one who did such a thing knowingly.
—William Anderson, Captain Cook's
Surgeon aboard *The Resolution,* commenting on the effects of their visit to Tonga in July 1777, 18 months before visiting Hawai'i and knowingly bringing the same disease to the Hawaiian people.

CONTENTS

Publisher's Note	xi
Acknowledgments	xiii
Preface	xv

Part One: Before the Horror

I.	Two Centuries of Error	3
II.	Growth, Sustenance, and Collapse	32
III.	Some Likely Objections	59
	Notes	81

Part Two: Critical Commentary and Reply

Comment by Eleanor C. Nordyke	105
Comment by Robert C. Schmitt	114
Reply by David E. Stannard	122
Index	147

PUBLISHER'S NOTE

The Editorial Board of the Social Science Research Institute welcomes the opportunity to publish this work by David Stannard in the SSRI Monograph Series. While most of the previous works in this series have treated contemporary social issues, this volume, a social history of the Hawaiians, departs somewhat from that tradition. Although the focus is on pre-contact population, the message has important implications for our contemporary perceptions of the Hawaiian people and their history.

In treating his topic, Professor Stannard has taken an interdisciplinary approach to explore new sources of historical data, including the often neglected oral history of the Hawaiian people, which has been transmitted through a direct line of ancestors stretching back to the dawn of time. Bringing together data from archaeology, geography, and epidemiology, as well as diaries and ships' logs, the author has developed a strong case for revising the accepted theories about the early population of the Hawaiian Islands, and the impact of the *haole* intrusion. The SSRI gladly supports this cross-disciplinary approach to social science research.

The debate on the question of what things were really like in pre-contact Hawai'i does not end with this monograph. Although we may never get a complete and perfect picture, studies such as this one will help us to keep in touch with the past, and hence better understand the present. In this work, the author has presented very insightful interpretations of new information, which hopefully will lead to further inquiry and appreciation of the original settlers of these islands.

DONALD M. TOPPING
Publisher

ACKNOWLEDGMENTS

The following study was conducted as part of a larger project I am pursuing on the social, cultural, and political impact of the epidemiological holocaust that nearly destroyed the Hawaiian people in the wake of their contact with the West. That larger project is under contract with Oxford University Press and I am thus very grateful to my editor at Oxford, Sheldon Meyer, for permitting separate and advance publication of this monograph. I also would like to thank the American Council of Learned Societies, the Hawai'i Cultural Research Foundation, and the University of Hawai'i Social Science Research Institute for their research support.

In addition to the invited critical readings by Eleanor C. Nordyke and Robert C. Schmitt, appended to this volume, in draft form this essay was reviewed by a number of helpful readers and critics, including Stephen T. Boggs, Andrew and Oswald Bushnell, Michael L. Forman, John Dominis Holt, Joanne C. Scheder, Donald M. Topping, and—in particular detail—Matthew J. T. Spriggs. I also have benefitted from discussions of various aspects of the project with Richard Kekuni Blaisdell, Sara L. Collins, Bertel Davis, Reuell N. Denney, John M. Hardman, Nina D. P. Horio, Lilikalā Kame'eleihiwa, Joseph Kennedy, Marion Kelly, and Carol Silva. Everett A. Wingert provided important cartographic information on more than one occasion and the library staffs at the Hawai'i-Pacific Collection of the University of Hawai'i Library, the Hawaiian Mission Children's Society Library, the Hawai'i Medical Library, and the State of Hawai'i Archives were most helpful. Linda Cristobal prepared the bulk of the manuscript with skill and great patience, while Sandra Enoki (who never fails at anything) and her staff of assistants (Linda Lum, Gail Mijo and

Myra Sanehira) stoically put up with my endless last-minute changes.

Needless to say, given the speculative and controversial nature of my findings, none of the above individuals necessarily share all my conclusions. One who does (although she thinks I'm too conservative) is Haunani-Kay Trask. Despite a very crowded political and scholarly agenda of her own, she has listened patiently to more monologues than she ever wanted to hear on death, disease, and depopulation, invariably contributing important insights of her own. Her support was crucial to the completion of this study —as it will be to the larger work of which this is but a detailed, technical part.

D.E.S.

He'eia, O'ahu
October, 1988

PREFACE

Less than twenty-five years ago conventional scholarly opinion held—as it had for generations—that the pre-Columbian population of the Americas was somewhere between 8 and 14 million persons, with no more than a million in North America. Today's historians and anthropologists now commonly accept figures up to ten times as high—as many as ten million in North America, twenty-five million in central Mexico alone, and 90 to 112 million for the entire hemisphere.[1] If correct, such estimates mean that the population of the Americas in the 15th century was equal to that of Europe, including Russia, at the time. And the numbers keep climbing. To cite a single example, one of the pioneers in the hemispheric reassessment recently has argued that North America alone may have contained not 1 or 10 million people, but 18 million prior to European contact.[2]

With every passing year vastly higher estimates appear in the scholarly literature of so-called "pre-contact" native populations, from the Canadian forest and lake regions to the mountains and coasts of Peru.* Concomitant with these estimates, of course, is the mounting evidence of massive population collapse following Western contact. A good deal of controversy surrounds the technical details and the specific conclusions of many of these new estimates, but the larger analysis is now widely accepted, and the field itself is alive with intellectual ferment and previously unimagined scholarly sophistication.

---

*The conventional phrase describing native societies prior to their contact with the West as "pre-contact" is both inaccurate and implicitly demeaning to those societies in that it ignores as unimportant inter-cultural contacts that occurred before the arrival of the West. In this monograph, therefore, in referring to Hawai'i and the Pacific prior to Western contact I will use the more accurate phrase "pre-*haole*"—*haole* being the Hawaiian word for foreigner, with specific reference to Caucasians.

In contrast with their colleagues in the Americas, Pacific island scholars generally have been content to accept and simply re-state the old and traditional wisdom on this subject. In fact, to the very limited extent that they have challenged traditional estimates of the size of pre-*haole* island populations, Pacific island scholars have tended to reduce rather than increase earlier figures.[3] And occasionally they have done so with a determined ideological gusto. New Zealand historian K. R. Howe, for example, has called the idea of large pre-*haole* island populations, followed by massive post-*haole* collapse, a "racist" falsehood, propagated by " 'liberal' writers to assuage feelings of guilt." Howe's notions of racism and guilt here are more than a little odd: first, he says, those who accept the historical reality of this demographic disaster implicitly must consider the natives to have been inferior and "witless" people for allowing themselves to succumb to imported diseases against which they had no immunities (the same sort of "witlessness" presumably demonstrated by Europeans when they fell victim to the Black Death); second, he says, the idea of "massive depopulation" betrays an "inverted racism" against the West for alleging that it was the source of the new diseases—which, of course, it was. The tendentiousness of this argument is compounded by the fact that, in the same book in which it appears, Professor Howe casually mentions that the larger geographical area of his study—New Caledonia—at one point following Western contact suffered what he admits was a largely disease-induced "catastrophic decline" in population of nearly 50 percent in less than twenty years! Unfortunately, such muddled logic is now common among Pacific island scholars writing on this topic.[4]

Although in Hawai'i the discussion of these matters has not commonly been clouded by such sophism in defense of ideology, conventional demographic history has followed essentially the same minimalist path. Thus, the most authoritative estimates of the Hawaiian population prior to Western contact set the number at somewhere between 200,000 and 300,000—guesses that are among the lowest since the first Western estimate in 1779. Even more extreme was the recent work of another prominent Pacific demographer, Norma McArthur, that reportedly was heading toward the extraordinary conclusion that the pre-*haole* population of Hawai'i was less than 100,000; McArthur's death, however, cut short her research before it was complete and the details supporting her alleged analysis are not available.⁵

If one thing is clear from all this, it is that the American revolution in historical demography that began with Woodrow Borah and Sherburne Cook as much as fifty years ago—and that spread throughout the scholarly world with Henry Dobyns' famous 1966 essay synthesizing and extending various local and hemispheric estimates—has had virtually no effect on Pacific island scholarship to date. In fact, Pacific island historical demography remains largely in an arrested state similar to that of such scholarship in the Americas of several decades ago. One consequence of this is a continuing Pacific island parallel to the old myth of pre-Columbian America as a nearly vacant "virgin land," patiently awaiting Western penetration and conquest.

For some time now, however, the "virgin land" myth of America has been supplanted by a more realistic image: as historian Francis Jennings has phrased it, the American landscape as viewed by the early European settlers was already a "widowed land," having been shorn of its indigenous people by the epidemic diseases carried aboard the ships of the very first Western explorers.⁶ It is time for Pacific island scholars to take another look at their own long-settled ideas on this subject. For even the most preliminary reassessment—and the present essay pretends to do no more than that—suggests that a very large upward revision of pre-European Pacific island population estimates is in order. As for Hawai'i, it is likely that for two centuries the population estimates for the pre-*haole* era have been too low by a factor of at least two or three to one. In 1778, as we shall see, the population of Hawai'i was probably almost as large as it is today.

PART ONE
Before the Horror

I

Two Centuries of Error

Since the closing years of the 18th century, estimates of Hawai'i's population prior to European contact have been founded on little more than the individual writer's intuitive reaction to the first carefully recorded estimate by a Western observer—the estimate of Lieutenant James King, who was elevated to Captain soon after Captain James Cook's death in Hawai'i in 1779, and who completed the three volume narrative of Cook's seafaring saga. King made two estimates. The first was a conjectured "half a Million," noted in his journal following a brief survey of the general appearance of the individual Hawaiian islands in comparison with other parts of the Pacific.[1] The second estimate, more carefully and elaborately presented, appeared in print a few years later. It reduced the earlier figure to about 400,000. This latter estimate, which followed a fairly detailed description of what little King had seen of the islands—either by sailing past them or landing briefly on certain parts of them—deserves to be quoted in full because we soon will be scrutinizing some of its assumptions:

> [T]he interior parts of the country are entirely uninhabited; so that, if the number of the inhabitants along the coast be known, the whole will be pretty accurately determined. The other [point] is, that there are no towns of any considerable size, the habitations of the natives being pretty equally dispersed in small villages, round all their coasts. It is on this ground, that I shall venture at a rough calculation of the number of persons in this group of islands.
>
> The Bay of Karakakooa, in Owhyhee [Kealakekua on the island of Hawai'i], is three miles in extant, and contains four villages of about eighty houses each; upon an average, in all three hundred and twenty; besides a number of straggling houses; which may make the whole amount to three hundred and fifty. From the frequent opportunities I had of informing

myself on this head, I am convinced, that six persons to a house is a very moderate allowance; so that, on this calculation, the country about the bay contains two thousand one hundred souls. To these may be added, fifty families, or three hundred persons, which I conceive to be nearly the number employed in the interior parts of the country, amongst their plantations; making in all two thousand four hundred. If, therefore, this number be applied to the whole extent of coast round the island, deducting a quarter for the uninhabited parts, it will be found to contain one hundred and fifty thousand. By the same mode of calculation, the rest of the islands will be found to contain the following numbers:

Owhyhee [Hawai'i]	------	150,000
Mowee [Maui]	------	65,400
Woahoo [O'ahu]	------	60,200
Atooi [Kaua'i]	------	54,000
Morotoi [Moloka'i]	------	36,000
Oneeheow [Ni'ihau]	------	10,000
Renai [Lāna'i]	------	20,400
Oreehoua [Lehua]	------	4,000
Total of inhabitants		400,000

I am pretty confident, that, in this calculation, we have not exceeded the truth in the total amount.[2]

King's estimate was barely in print before it came under attack. It seemed "greatly exaggerated," wrote Captain George Dixon, who visited Hawai'i in 1787. Dixon thought 200,000 might be a closer approximation. And William Bligh, soon to become the legendary commander of the *Bounty*, scribbled a cryptic (and unexplained) estimate of 242,200 as a result of his observations while aboard the *Resolution* during Cook's last voyage.[3]

Later writers took various positions on King's estimate, some supporting it, some criticizing it. But almost none of them produced any evidence or analysis to support their positions. As Robert C. Schmitt, the Hawai'i State Statistician and currently the reigning authority on the past and present populations of Hawai'i has put it: "None of these precensal estimates is very convincing. Methodology typically remains unstated, and even where described it is questionable." In producing his own estimate (at present the most quoted and widely accepted) Schmitt seems to have assumed without question that King's figure of 400,000 was the highest number possible; from that unargued assumption Schmitt then proceeds to draw on the critiques of Dixon, Bligh, and others as a way of whittling King's estimate down to what he considers more acceptable size. In addition to Dixon and Bligh on the 1778 population, for example, Schmitt points out that the Russian Captain V. M. Golovnin visited Hawai'i in 1818 and, like Dixon, came up with a 1778 figure of 200,000, "citing the opinion of European residents as his authority."[4] Moreover, Schmitt notes:

> These lower figures are given partial support by contemporary evidence for individual islands. Both Dixon and [Archibald] Menzies visited Kaua'i during the eighteenth century and found King's estimate (and perhaps Cook's) too high. William Bayly hiked over two-thirds of Ni'ihau on January 29, 1778 and reported only one-twentieth the population later estimated by King. [Captain George] Vancouver and Menzies noted that Lehua, said by King to have 4,000 inhabitants, was unpopulated. [Kenneth] Emory's archeological survey of Lāna'i indicated a maximum pre-contact population of 3,150, in contrast to King's estimate of 20,400.[5]

Putting all this together, while acknowledging that "the evidence . . . is admittedly sketchy and judgment plays an uncomfortably large role," Schmitt concluded his authoritative 1971 study with a stab in the dark estimate that "the 1778 population of the Hawaiian islands was not over 250,000, and possibly as low as 200,000." Schmitt subsequently has admitted that this range may be too low, but he still contends that the population did not exceed 300,000 and probably was a good deal less. Interestingly, although his is the most careful work on this subject to date, Schmitt's present conclusion is precisely the same as that of previous writers he has criticized for basing their estimates "on evidence of the flimsiest kind."[6]

Among Schmitt's undoubted axioms, particularly as regards King's estimates, is the belief that "a high degree of overestimation" is common in early travelers' estimates and that "demographers have observed, for example, that 'the depletion of primitive peoples has probably been exaggerated in many cases,' by the natives themselves as well as by navigators, missionaries, and administrators." Unfortunately, Schmitt's source for this sweeping remark about "primitive peoples" is not "demographers," in the plural, but merely one of the dwindling handful of holdouts—demographer William Petersen—who persist in denying the demonstrated reality of the great Indian population collapse in the Americas, the catastrophe that most authorities now accept as probably the worst demographic disaster in the history of the world.⁷ In fact, the reality that has become apparent to virtually all historical demographers and anthropologists in the past few decades, whatever their views on specific peoples or problems, is the precise opposite of what Schmitt and most early writers have contended; as Henry Dobyns, among many others, has shown: "Ethnohistorical estimations based on careful cross-checking of direct and indirect sources of population data demonstrate that contemporary observers *underreported* the true magnitude of native American populations."⁸

But what of the specific contradictions of King that Schmitt cites from contemporary sources—that is, Bligh, Dixon, Menzies, Golovnin, Bayly, and Vancouver? The veracity of these writings is the *entire* foundation upon which Schmitt's critique of King, and Schmitt's own eventual estimate, is built. As they go, so goes his argument. This is a crucial point that cannot be overemphasized: without believable support from these sources, *no* data or argument remain to support Schmitt's estimate. It's credibility simply vanishes and we return to square one. We must, therefore, examine these references carefully, one at a time. First the all-island estimates cited by Schmitt:

—Bligh's estimate cannot be dealt with at all (as Schmitt essentially admits) because there are no data given to support it. Bligh never published it and, for all its pseudo-precision, it appears to have been plucked from thin air—to which it deserves to be returned.

—Dixon's estimate is based entirely upon his observations at Waimea Bay on the island of Kaua'i *eight years after* King's observations and estimates were made. His procedure apparently (it is unstated) was to note that the district of Waimea's population appeared at that time to be about half of what King had earlier thought it to be; thus, he reasoned, the population of the rest of Kaua'i must also be about half King's estimate; and, indeed, this same generalization must therefore hold for the population of the entire archipelago. Apart from the crudity of this procedure (Dixon himself admits that his "acquaintance with the major part of [the islands] is very superficial") Dixon also records, Schmitt fails to note, evidence of the contagious diseases that the *Resolution* and *Discovery* had left at Waimea Bay almost a decade earlier. For instance, Dixon notes that the nephew of a chief, a young man whose physique he had "greatly admired" during a visit only nine months earlier (the young man and others were "by far the finest men we had yet seen at any of the islands") was now grown heavy and his skin was covered with "scurf." When Dixon asked the young man if the condition was the result of drinking 'awa (a mildly intoxicating herbal drink common in the Pacific and just as commonly—and indiscriminately—blamed for every imaginable ill by early Western observers), the young man replied that he was too young to be allowed to drink 'awa, that the condition derived from something else—unknown—and that it was "breaking out very common amongst them." While we shall never know with assurance what the young man's affliction was (it is common for newly-introduced diseases to manifest themselves differently in a population without acquired immunities) we do know that Cook's ships, and probably Dixon's as well, brought both syphilis and tuberculosis to Hawai'i. As well as the beginnings of secondary syphilis, the symptoms described by Dixon might have been a form of cutaneous tuberculosis or scrofuloderma resulting from tuberculosis of the lymph node (commonly called scrofula) which later became noted in European medical circles for its particularly destructive effects on Pacific island children.[9] And, as we shall see later, tuberculosis introduced into previously uninfected populations has been known to cause 50 percent mortality in less than a decade.

In any case, whatever the specific diagnosis, not only is Dixon's "correction" of King based on the narrowest and flimsiest of grounds, as Dixon himself acknowledged, it also contains clear evidence—supported by virtually every other visitor during this same time—of a crucial matter we will discuss shortly: the disease and consequent severe depopulation that began sweeping through the Hawaiian Islands even before the departure of Cook's ships, the results of which were no doubt reflected in Dixon's casual observations at Waimea.

—Golovnin's 1818 all-island estimate of 200,000 was not, as Schmitt claims, an estimate of the 1778 population; rather, it was a contemporary report of residents' estimates of the *1818* population by a man who incorrectly assumed the number to have been unchanged since 1778. (At one point, for example, Golovnin blithely states that "epidemics and infections are unknown to the inhabitants" of Hawai'i, while even the most conservative modern estimates—Schmitt's for example—admit that by 1818 the native population was barely half its 1778 level.)[10] In brief, as a careful reading of Golovnin's text will show, he was writing in the *present tense* (1818)—while ignorant of the epidemiological history of Hawai'i's past forty years. To that extent his report, based on the estimates of "the Europeans living there," was probably fairly correct: in 1818 there were at least 200,000 people living in Hawai'i.[11] But 1778 was a far different story.

As for the alleged corrections of King based on individual island surveys:

—Dixon's Kaua'i estimate is discussed above.

—Menzies' report on his 1792–93 visit to Kaua'i containing the supposed correction of King refers not only to Kaua'i, but also to Ni'ihau. However, although Schmitt does not mention it, the cited comment by Menzies is immediately followed by this sentence: "But as many of the natives may probably be now absent on the present warlike expedition against Hawai'i, it is reasonable to think that anything now offered on the subject with respect to the Leeward Islands in particular [which include Kaua'i and Ni'ihau] may not be a fair inference."[12] And still later Menzies remarks that another of King's estimates may be "an exaggerated calculation, *or the population since his time must be greatly diminished on all the islands*."[13] As we shall soon see, in addition to Menzies' accurate qualifier regarding the ongoing warfare (which was also true when Dixon made his 1786–87 estimates) his later suspicion that the population had been sharply reduced during the previous decade and a half was indeed correct.

—Schmitt is wrong in his assertion that "William Bayly hiked over two-thirds of Ni'ihau on January 29, 1778." Bayly's journal does not say that he hiked "*over* two-thirds" of the island, which would indicate an area of almost fifty square miles walked in a single day; rather, it says that "at daylight [on the 30th] I went ashore and traveled about 2/3 of the length of the island." However, Bayly thought the island to be "about 10 or 11 miles long and about 3 1/2 miles broad," an estimate that is too small almost by half. What Bayly's journal *in fact* reports, then, is that he walked into the island—starting, it must be noted, from its most arid, least habitable side—about six miles, then turned around and walked back. During this jaunt, he saw (to be generous) perhaps ten percent of the island's surface, and the dryest and least cultivable ten percent at that (not the 65 to 70 percent that Schmitt's language suggests); he also saw there "a number of little towns" along with a good deal of land planted in yams and sweet potatoes as well as "fine groves of sugar cane." From this very small and unrepresentative observation, Bayly estimated the island's population at about 500.[14]

Bayly's mistake, therefore, is understandable. But we have information that he did not. What Bayly missed on his brief tour was the entire upland region of the island. This area, which constitutes about half the island's surface, vividly contrasts with the sandy lowland that he saw in its high-oxide soil quality (its Oxisol soil is the most important agricultural soil classification in Hawai'i) and its rainfall, which, even today, when it probably is substantially lower than in pre-*haole* times, is as much as double the amount common in the lowland. No doubt this is why Ni'ihau —which not only King, but others, found "thick inhabited" and filled with "many inhabitants"—produced such an "immense quantity of yams and sugar cane" that Cook's crew loaded at that stop enough provisions to feed almost 200 sailors for two to three months at sea.[15] Subsequent ships did the same thing; for example, on just one day in 1786 Captain Nathaniel Portlock had 18 *tons* of yams (and nearly a ton of pork) loaded on board his two ships during a stopover at Ni'ihau. Indeed, as Portlock notes, Kaumuhonu Bay at the southern tip of Ni'ihau became known as "Yam Bay" to 18th century explorers, virtually all of whom made a point of stopping there because of the incredible amounts of yams produced and available for trade.[16] To be sure, Ni'ihau was never as agriculturally productive as the other, much larger, islands, and it was probably susceptible to occasionally serious droughts; but whatever the population of the island, its level of agricultural production shows that it was far from small—though it was concentrated in areas unseen by Bayly.

—Vancouver and Menzies were no doubt correct in stating that the tiny island of Lehua was essentially uninhabited, rather than containing the 4000 people that King's estimate projected. On the other hand, King made no population estimate for the island of

Kahoʻolawe. The channel between Kahoʻolawe and Maui was too dangerous for any of the early ships to sail through, although that hidden side of the island produced significant crops of sweet potatoes and sugar cane, while supporting a definite though numerically unknown population.[17] So the minor deduction for Lehua from King's total estimate is at least partially compensated for by the addition of Kahoʻolawe's population.

For those who are familiar with 20th century Hawaiʻi and who might dispute these observations based on contemporary appearances, it is worth remembering that neither Niʻihau nor Kahoʻolawe were as arid in pre-*haole* times as they are today. The post-*haole* introduction of grazing animals and the consequent destruction of vegetation on both islands not only resulted in massive topsoil erosion, but also altered the delicate climatic balance of the islands: surface and sub-surface temperatures are markedly higher today than they were in pre-*haole* times, rainfall is lighter, near-surface winds are substantially stronger, and the remaining soil is much dryer and more susceptible to runoff than to infiltration. The same situation holds for other parts of Hawaiʻi that were victimized by the post-*haole* grazing of introduced animals. On the island of Hawaiʻi, for example, huge tracts of once fertile and cultivated land had been reduced by the end of the 19th century to what one traveler described as "a worthless dusty desert" as a result of careless post-*haole* overgrazing. And since the end of the 19th century the situation has grown worse, with measured rainfall in this area having declined by as much as 40 percent during the course of the 20th century. Still, even today, when viewed from high ground or from the air, the ancient grid lines of this long-destroyed vast agricultural field system cast their shadows in the afternoon light.[18]

—Finally, Kenneth Emory's archaeological survey of the island of Lānaʻi does indeed project a pre-*haole* population of just under 3200 people, though Emory also makes several other observations, not noted by Schmitt, that deserve mention. For instance, Emory quotes the 1793 comment of one Hawaiian chief (*via* Captain Vancouver) that before 1778 both Lānaʻi and Kahoʻolawe had been "fruitful and populous islands" that in just 15 years had become "nearly overrun with weeds, and exhausted of their inhabitants." Emory also points out that his pre-*haole* population estimate is based on a count of house sites on the island; but in the area where the population would have been most heavily concentrated by far (the coastal plain of the island's windward side) there are the fewest number of house sites visible today because the favorable topography did not require the platform or enclosure construction common in the less habitable areas. Emory tries to compensate for this by making the unrealistically conservative guess that there may have been "twice as many houses as house sites noted on the plateau lands" and comments that the resultant total, which includes some other speculative adjustments, is probably "not an overestimate." Indeed, it almost certainly was a gross underestimate, since Emory later notes:

> This much is certain, Lāna'i was inhabited to such an extent that even the most inhospitable regions show ruins of house platforms, bluff dwellings and garden patches. Since all natural features were taken advantage of as dwelling sites, during periods of maximum population doubtless all the house sites except those under a tapu, were occupied.[19]

The fact that "even the most inhospitable regions" were inhabited (something, as we shall see, that was common among the islands) conforms with the native observation that, before 1778, the island was "fruitful and populous." It also supports the earliest Western observation, by King, that "the Island look'd very Pleasant, and the borders seemed full of Villages"—and note that King saw at relatively close range only one of the most arid parts of the island. (The part of the island Cook's ships approached most closely, for example, the area around the village of Kaunolū, is in a locale that receives only about 10 inches of rainfall per year.) If Emory's guess of a pre-*haole* population of 3200 were correct, the resulting population density of Lana'i would be less than 23 people per square mile—barely half the population density of the state of Oklahoma today or a little more than double that of baboons in the wild—hardly "populous", hardly "full of Villages," and hardly dense enough to require habitation of "even the most inhospitable regions," including drought-plagued Ka'ena Point, where the largest *heiau* on the island is located.[20]

Moreover, Lāna'i's population in the mid-1820s was estimated at the time to be as high as 3000, and indirect evidence suggests it may have been double that figure.[21] If it was 3000 at that time, and we assume the lowest possible 1778–1823 rate of depopulation, the *minimum* 1778 population would project back to between 5000 and 6000 people. However, since Lāna'i (along with Kaho'olawe) was devasted almost immediately after 1778—as Vancouver's writings show—its population decline would have been much more precipitous than the all-island rate. A pre-*haole* figure of 10,000 to 12,000 would be a reasonable estimate, and still possibly well short of the mark. If the 1823 population was in fact around 6000 (see note 21) the 1778 population could easily have equalled or surpassed King's estimate of 20,400.

Nevertheless, on this general matter Schmitt may have a point: King's straight-line, coastal mile projection method could have overestimated the population of some of the smaller islands. On the other hand, it most certainly greatly underestimated the population of the major islands, so any minor correction for the smallest islands—especially in view of everything else discussed above—hardly damages King's all-island estimate. In fact, if we tentatively assume—as Schmitt does at one point—that the population *ratios* of the various islands to the all-island total were roughly the same in 1778 as they were in the first genuine census of 1831–32, King's breakdown would be corrected approximately as follows:

	King's 1778 estimate	Corrected to conform to 1831–32 ratio	Adjusted population per square mile
Hawai'i	150,000	140,000	34.7
Maui	65,400	108,000	148.2
O'ahu	60,200	91,400	150.4
Kaua'i	54,000	34,000	61.4
Moloka'i	36,000	18,400	70.5
Lāna'i	20,400	5,000	35.9
Ni'ihau	10,000	3,200	43.8
Lehua	4,000		
Kaho'olawe			
Total	400,000	400,000	62.0

With just this small and logical preliminary adjustment the quibblings over the populations of Lāna'i, Ni'ihau, and Lehua lose whatever little force they had, while King's all-island figure remains the same. As for the larger figures for Maui and O'ahu (neither of which were seen at close range by King), the *higher* populations for those islands compute to population densities that, as we shall see, were much *lower* than the probable densities of the Marquesas Islands and a bit higher than Tahiti—the most closely related islands to Hawai'i—at the time of Western contact. So they are hardly unrealistically high figures. Indeed, it is the unrealistically *low* density figures for the other islands (especially Hawai'i, Kaua'i, and Moloka'i) that seem problematic.

Moreover, while it is commonly known that at least 10,000 to 15,000 people were in canoes and swimming in the island of Hawai'i's Kealakekua Bay during the first afternoon of Cook's visit there (while, at the same time, wrote John Ledyard, "the crouds on shore were still more numerous"—as, added Cook, "all the Shore of the bay was covered with people") what is often overlooked is the fact that a similar number were on shore at Waimea on Kaua'i when the ships stopped there on their departure from the islands. One day, wrote David Samwell, "no less than ten or twelve thousand" appeared.[22] This figure (representing between one-half and nearly two-thirds of Schmitt's lower estimate for the entire population of Kaua'i) would mean, if Schmitt's archipelagic population estimate were correct, that between 15 and 20 percent of the population of *all* the Hawaiian islands, with their highly labor-intensive economies, happened to be lolling about the beaches at just these two small and relatively arid locations—separated from one another by 300 miles of ocean—when Cook's ships stopped by. While there is no doubt that a large number of nonresidents would have been drawn from neighboring districts to these locales out of curiosity and, in the case of Kealakekua Bay, because of a major religious ceremony *(Makahiki)* that was then in progress, it is highly unlikely that such high *percentages* of the individual or all-island populations would have been there. The single island of Hawai'i, after all, is over 4000 square miles in size —nearly double the combined size of the dozens of islands that comprise Tonga, the Marquesas, the Society Islands (including Tahiti), and Western and American Sāmoa. Those 30,000 to 40,000 natives in the water and on the beaches at Kealakekua and Waimea in fact must have represented much less than 15 to 20 percent of what had to be a vastly larger archipelagic population than Schmitt contends.

None of this is to say that if Schmitt's estimate is wrong, King's estimate was necessarily correct. It most certainly was not. The point here simply is that all efforts to date (including Schmitt's) to *reduce* King's estimate are sorely lacking in evidentiary or even logical support. King's estimate is indeed quite subject to criticism, but from the opposite direction: the figure of 400,000 was far too small. To recognize this, we must turn to the assumptions King acknowledged as the underpinnings of his estimate:

1. He thought the population of Kealakekua Bay was about 2400 persons, making for a population density of 800 persons per coastal mile.
2. He thought the population density of Kealakekua Bay was approximately the same as that prevailing along the entire inhabited coastline of all the Hawaiian islands.
3. He believed that about a quarter of all the islands' coastlines were uninhabited.
4. He thought that only the coastlines were inhabited, that there was no inland population.

Let us examine these assumptions in order.

1. King acknowledged that his estimate of the population along the coast of Kealakekua Bay may have been too small, based as it was on what he properly called the "very moderate allowance" of six persons living per house and a house count of 350 residences, plus a guess of fifty houses "among the plantations." In fact, house-counting in this sort of cultural and environmental setting as a way of estimating resident population is almost bound to result in an undercount; for example, the *Resolution*'s surgeon, John Law, observed "many people" living in caves on the cliffs north of the bay, the openings of which had "scantling of woods placed before the Holes making a Small Door or Entrance into them, and Ladders fixed to the rocks from one Hole to the other." His description clearly suggests that these were not burial caves, but, as he put it, were residences "Inhabited by the poorer kind of People." Beyond that, however, both of King's figures—for number of houses and for number of persons per house—may have been too low. This can be of minor consequence for the local population estimate, but has a major impact on the all-island figure

that is extrapolated from it. As for the number of houses, David Samwell counted 370 to 380 houses in the same area that King found 350. John Ledyard, in perhaps the most detailed discussion of the subject, found 1100 houses ("some reckon 1300 including some detached buildings") in the space of a mile and a half—that is, about three and a half times as many houses in half the space that King reported. Midshipman George Gilbert referred to the villages around the bay as "at least eight times as big as any we had seen before in the south sea," adding that "the Country here is one entire plantation," stretching "as far as we could see from the ship." And the *Discovery*'s Captain Charles Clerke, after acknowledging that many of the people assembled on shore had come from other areas, nevertheless wrote that "the immense number of Men and women *living* in the various villages about this Bay surpassed every idea of populousness I could ever form."[23]

It is difficult to account for the great discrepancy in house counts between King and Ledyard, except for the possibility that Ledyard may have been including all housing structures in his account and it is known that, because of the *kapu* system, Hawaiian households were not commonly confined to a single structure. Since King, who invariably is cautious in reporting his observations and conclusions, makes a point of noting the "frequent opportunities I had of informing myself" on the matter of household size, it seems probable that his figure, supported by the slightly larger calculation of the equally careful Samwell, was more accurate than that of Ledyard.

As for the number of inhabitants per house, even after half a century of drastic depopulation—especially in the number of children per family—Western observers, such as the missionary printer and teacher Elisha Loomis, witnessed and slept in houses south of Kealakekua that were considerably smaller than those described by King, but that contained nearly double the number of people. (In 1778-79 the houses observed on both Kaua'i and Hawai'i ranged from "little huts" perhaps twenty feet long and twelve feet wide to larger homes "from forty or fifty feet long and twenty or thirty broad"; in 1824 Loomis found buildings ten feet by ten feet that housed eleven people.) Others of Cook's crew in 1779 found "many larger" houses that contained "two or three families each" within walking distance of Kealakekua Bay. Just up the same coastline, in the district of Kohala, there exist today the remains of inland pre-*haole* dwellings substantially larger than many of those described at Kealakekua Bay. And the *Missionary Herald*, in 1823—when, again, the population and probable household size was vastly reduced from that of 1778—reported an average household size of eight persons, compared with King's self-admitted "very moderate allowance" of six.[24]

In fact, King's population counts were almost always on the conservative side. For example, on that famous day of January 17, 1779, when the *Discovery* and *Resolution* entered Kealakekua Bay and were surrounded by more people than Cook or any of his men had ever, in all their voyages, seen assembled at one place, King estimated the number of canoes at "not less than 15 hundred." In contrast, John Rickman estimated "not less than 2 or 3000" and Ledyard—after reporting on two "official" counts of over 3000 by Cook's officers—noted "I shall say with safety there was 2500."[25]

Moreover, as Schmitt acknowledges, an 1822 population count of the same area found an average of 685 people per mile of coastline. Another count in 1823 found what computes to an average of 623 people per coastal mile among the "thickly scattered" villages between Keauhou and Kailua—a bit up the coast from Kealakekua Bay. These figures are, respectively, less than 15 percent and 22 percent lower than King's 1778 estimate of coastal population density, while even the most conservative calculations set the all-island depopulation rate by 1822 at 40 to 50 percent. In fact, barely fifteen miles away from the site of King's 1778 estimate, a count in 1823 recorded nearly 3000 people residing along a single mile of coastline at the village of Kailua—that is, almost four times the coastal density estimated by King forty-five years earlier—despite the area being "destitute of fresh water."[26] These counts in the 1820s were made not only long after the population had begun its catastrophic collapse, but also after the death of King Kamehameha, who had made a practice in the post-*haole* era of gathering his chiefs around him in this area, so there is no reason to suppose that activity would have inflated the latter numbers. Indeed, unless there is good reason to hold that Kealakekua Bay and its surrounding areas were miraculously protected from the biological devastation that struck virtually everywhere else in the islands—and there is none—we must conclude that King's 1779 estimate of the permanent population at Kealakekua Bay was a substantial underestimate.

2. King's assumption that the population density of Kealakekua Bay was the same along all the islands' inhabited coastlines is a serious error with substantial consequences. Kealakekua Bay, like Kaua'i's Waimea Bay—the *only* two places in Hawai'i where King spent any time ashore—is on the leeward side of the island, surrounded by a huge and notoriously dry landscape. To be sure, the area immediately around Kealakekua Bay was heavily cultivated by virtue of the Hawaiians' remarkable agricultural skills, combined with certain climatic conditions unique to this particular leeward locale (including fog and late afternoon clouds and showers); and Waimea, on Kaua'i, was made more fertile than it otherwise would have been by the presence of the Waimea River. But in general the Hawaiian islands were no exception to the demographic and common-sense rule that populations are largest in those areas with the greatest fresh water supply. And if there was one thing that was lacking at Kealakekua Bay, compared with other parts of the island of Hawai'i and other islands in the Hawaiian chain, it was abundant fresh water. In fact, it was primarily because the water they had taken on board at Kealakekua Bay was so "very brackish and bad" that the *Resolution* and *Discovery* headed for Maui on their aborted departure from the islands on February 6, 1779, and had to make what their officers feared might be a dangerous stop at Kaua'i upon their actual departure in March.[27]

The Hawaiians, no doubt, had long grown more accustomed to sustaining themselves on brackish drinking water than the visiting Englishmen could, but the fact remains that the greatest concentrations of population were found in the areas with the greatest concentrations of fresh water. And in the Hawaiian islands— where, tellingly, the indigenous word for "water" is *wai* and the word for "wealthy" is *waiwai*—the greatest fresh water supplies are invariably found in the windward areas. For example, on the island of Hawai'i, Hilo (windward) receives nearly three and a half times the mean annual rainfall that Kailua (leeward) does, and more than sixteen times what Puakō (leeward) does; on Maui, Hāna (windward) receives nearly five and a half times the rainfall that Lahaina (leeward) does; on Kaua'i, Kīlauea (windward) receives nearly three and a half times what Waimea (leeward) does; and on Oʻahu, Kahana (windward) receives more than twelve times the rainfall that Mākaha (leeward) does.

Cook's ships were unable to approach the shore during their trip around the island of Hawaiʻi's windward coast, although the Hawaiians could row out to the ships. This was true of all the islands—and for very good navigational reasons: prevailing winds blowing toward the land from the northeast make it very dangerous to sail close to the lee shore (the windward coast) of an island, particularly if one is sailing in unfamiliar waters. Thus, it was standard practice to stay at a safe distance from the windward coastlines, limiting close-to-shore sailing and landings to the navigationally safer leeward coasts. But, despite their restricted views of Hawaiʻi's windward areas, the accounts of those on board Cook's two ships are alive with observations of throngs of people greeting them from the shoreline and trading with them from their canoes all the way across and down the island's northern and eastern (windward) coasts. The first parts of the island that were sighted—the immense northernmost windward valleys from Pololū and Honokāne to Waipiʻo, which today are almost totally uninhabited but at the time were terraced and farmed by large populations—were "very rich and fertile," wrote the *Discovery's* Captain Clerke; they were "fully" and "entirely" cultivated, added King. In this area they were greeted by "thousands of people [who] collected together to look at the ships," noted Samwell. And day after day in this area, Cook wrote, they "procured pork, fruit and roots" in large quantities from native traders in their canoes. Later, the hills along the Hāmākua (north-east windward) coast "were almost covered" with people, observed the *Discovery's* surgeon's second mate William Ellis; such "great numbers" of men and women sailed out to greet and trade with the ships as they made their way down the coast, wrote Samwell, that "during the whole time of trafficking with them it is nothing but one scene of noise & confusion on board the ships & all round them." Further south, off the district of Hilo, King found the "cultivation and villages are equal to Amacooa [Hāmākua]." And Puna, the windward district immediately south of Hilo, King said, was "a very fine part of the island, perhaps the best," because, added Samwell, it was an area with "the most fertile & pleasant appearance . . . being almost entirely covered with Groves of Cocoa nut & other fruit trees" among which there lived "many people" in houses erected on platforms near the sea. (Subsequently, it should be noted, much of the Puna district that so impressed King and Samwell and the others has become covered with lava from volcanic eruptions.) In fact, so populous and well-provisioned was the windward side of the island, said George Gilbert, that the "great numbers" of natives they encountered down the coast commonly gave the ships, with their nearly 200 men aboard, "provisions enough for five or six days . . . in three or four hours and [we] might have got three times as much if we had chose, for the greater part of the Canoes" —often 200 at a time, observed Rickman—"were obliged to return to shore with what they had brought off to us."[28]

The importance of fresh water for population support is, of course, not limited to its use as drinking water. One of the achievements of the ancient Hawaiians that permitted the support of what we shall soon see was a huge population was the development of large-scale terraces and irrigated fields for the growing of taro, the staple of the Hawaiian diet. And it was the windward sides of the major islands that were the locations of these extremely sophisticated agricultural complexes.[29] Indeed, not only was there a good deal more water available in the windward areas, but (and this is crucial) the reliability of rainfall was greater because there is a positive correlation between the amount and the reliability of precipitation: the higher the mean annual amount, the higher the reliability; the lower the mean annual amount, the lower the reliability.[30] Thus, in archaeologist Robert J. Hommon's words:

> The predominance of intermittent streams, prone to flash flooding is particularly characteristic of the younger islands [the island of Hawai'i is the youngest of the Hawaiian islands] and leeward portions of individual islands. Mature valleys with broad floors, low gradients, and permanent streams are most abundant on the older islands and in the older and windward portions of individual islands. The soils in these valleys are alluvial in nature, which tend to be relatively impermeable and rich in organic content.[31]

These older and windward valleys, as the sites of large-scale irrigation, were able to support much larger permanent popula-

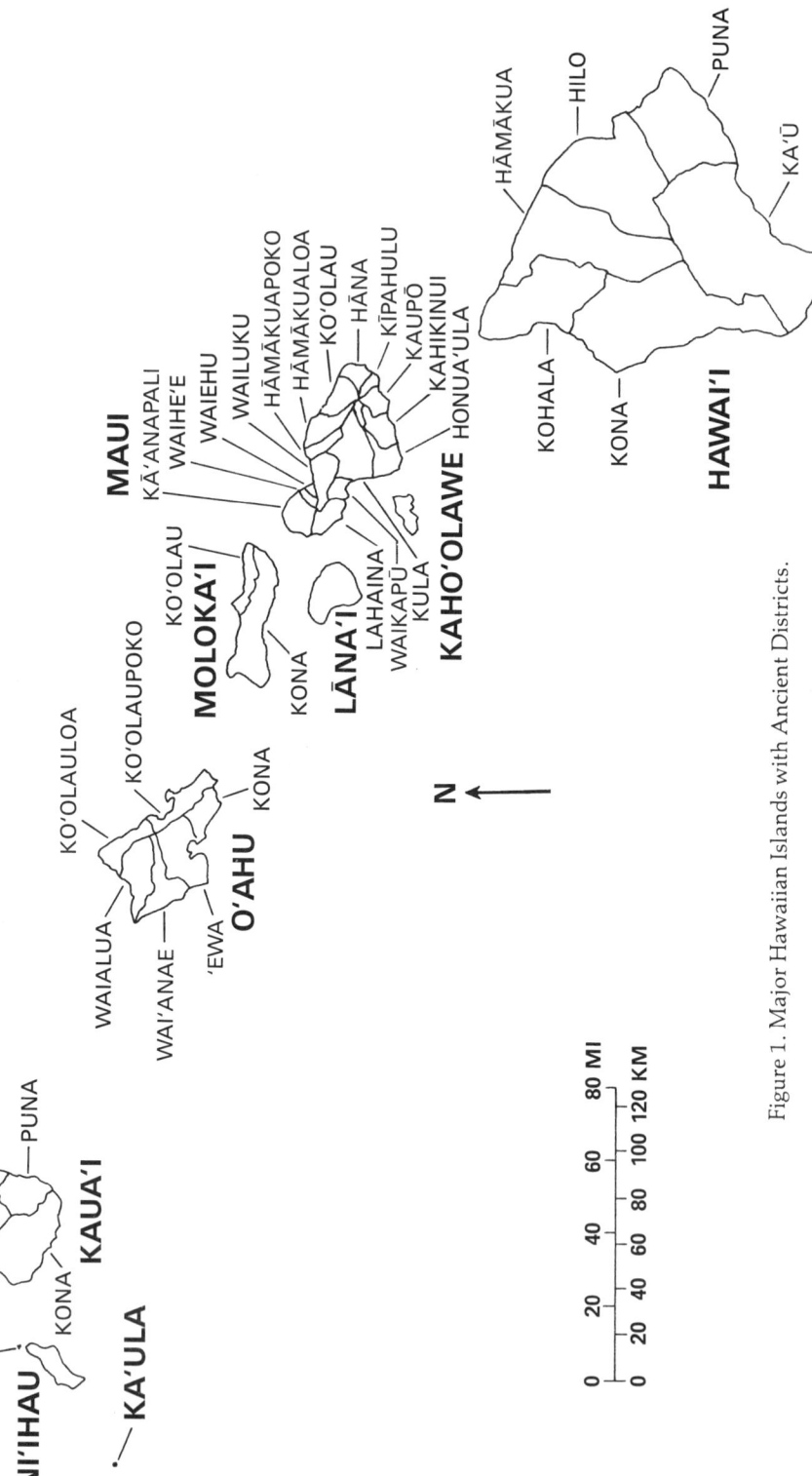

Figure 1. Major Hawaiian Islands with Ancient Districts.

tion densities than could the younger islands and the leeward areas in general because the irrigated fields were farmed almost continuously. And it is now known, from studies of desert areas that have been irrigated, that rainfall amounts actually increase immediately downwind of irrigated areas and that agriculturally favorable temperature and barometric pressure changes also occur—thus multiplying the already favorable conditions for habitation. In contrast, the non-irrigated growing areas on the leeward sides of the islands had to be allowed to go fallow for five or ten years at a time. "In some areas," writes archaeologist T. Stell Newman, "this simply meant abandoning a growing area when it showed a poor crop return and clearing a new one, often by fire, from the surrounding forest. In other areas the fields were formalized into field systems, with some fields used while others lay fallow before being replanted and used again."[32] In either case, the requirements of non-irrigated farming necessitated a much larger area to support the same population that existed in smaller areas with irrigated farming. A recent study by anthropologist Marion Kelly makes this point dramatically:

> An acre of irrigated pondfields produced as much as five times the amount of taro as an acre of dry-land cultivation. Over a period of several years, irrigated pondfields could be as much as *10 or 15 times* more productive than unirrigated taro gardens, as dry-land gardens need to lie fallow for greater lengths of time than irrigated gardens.[33]

It is thus not mere coincidence that, of the traditional land divisions on the island of Hawai'i, the district of Kona (the district in which Kealakekua Bay is located) and the district of Ka'ū take up almost as much land area as the combined size of the other four districts on the island. That is because these two dry districts on the leeward side of the youngest island, large as their populations were, were unable to support the extraordinary population *densities* that prevailed on the older islands and—on the island of Hawai'i—in the windward districts of Hāmākua, Hilo, and Puna, or perhaps even the northern leeward district of Kohala, which had many times the arable land area of Kona. Indeed, on every major island the largest geographic district is also the driest and least easily habitable: Ka'ū on Hawai'i, Kula on Maui, Kona on Moloka'i, 'Ewa on O'ahu, and Kona on Kaua'i. [See Figure 1]

Another way to think about this matter of windward/leeward population distribution is to consider the fact that political rivalry and sometimes armed conflict were common on the island of Hawai'i, with the leeward districts of Kona, Ka'ū, and Kohala traditionally allied against the windward districts of Hilo, Hāmākua, and Puna. Despite this, permanent conquest by either side never occurred; indeed, the windward chiefs usually prevailed in battle, suggesting at the least a long-term balance of power, with a general tilt in favor of the geographically smaller windward districts. Given the limited pre-*haole* military technology, this distribution of power was, of course, also a reflection of population distribution, as Henry Dobyns has shown in his study of the Indian populations of northern Florida and southeastern Georgia in the late 16th century.[34] However, if (as King assumed) the windward population had been distributed with the same density per coastal mile as the leeward population, the windward districts would have suffered a fatal 60 to 40 military and population disadvantage.[35] In short, because of their comparatively small size, the windward districts *had* to have a much higher population density than the leeward districts in order for population and relative military parity to be sustained.

But King did not see the island of Hawaii's windward districts at close range. And on Kaua'i his only landing was in the heart of the one district (Kona) that was so arid and thinly populated relative to other areas that it occupied nearly the same land area as all the other four districts on the island combined. [See Figure 1] Ironically, although King would never have guessed it from what he saw of the island, relative to its size Kaua'i had a far greater supply of permanent fresh water—in streams and rivers—than any of the other Hawaiian islands. Given the very limited and unrepresentative parts of Hawai'i and Kaua'i that King was able to see at close range, then, it was inevitable that he would underestimate significantly both islands' populations.

Again, on both Kaua'i and Hawai'i, the English did visit specific leeward areas that were more cultivable and thus more densely populated than much of the rest of the leeward coastline; and it was from one of these locales that King made the population count that served as the model for his all-island extrapolations. But if these particular small areas were more densely populated than the average leeward coastal locations, they were also much *less* densely populated than the windward areas.

As it turned out, in fact, because of the necessity for sailing ships to concentrate their movements on the leeward sides of the islands, Cook's ships missed seeing the heavy population areas on all the islands they observed: in addition to viewing closely only the leeward sides of Kaua'i and Hawai'i, they missed all of O'ahu —which contains almost half the prime agricultural land in the archipelago—with the exception of a small part of the north shore (where, in their hurry to leave, the men "lamented" having to miss visiting what they described as the finest island they had ever encountered, with its "many large Villages and extensive plantations"); they completely missed the densely populated (in pre-*haole* times) eastern coast of Maui, from Ke'anae to Hāna and Kīpahulu (where the largest religious shrine in all of Oceania had been constructed by that enormous population); and they saw almost nothing of Moloka'i which, with only 4 percent of the all-island land mass, was heavily cultivated on its windward side and, on its southern coast, contained at least 16 percent of all the islands' hundreds of huge, man-made fish ponds, from which millions of pounds of specially grown fish were harvested each year— millions of pounds of fish that were produced by an ingenious and unique aquacultural technique that multiplied by *100 times* the natural food chain efficiency of protein production.[36]

Considering his extremely limited and unbalanced views of the islands, it is not surprising that King might assume that the undeniably impressive population density of Kealakekua Bay was safely representative of all the inhabited coasts of Hawai'i. But we should know better. After all, the explorers subsequent to Cook and King did. As the French captain J. F. G. de la Pérouse plainly noted in his journal of May 1786: "In these islands, the most fertile and healthy districts, and consequently the most populous, are always to the windward."[37]

3. Another understandable mistake made by King that lowered unrealistically his all-island population estimate was his assumption that a quarter of all the islands' coastlines were uninhabited. The only island King got even a reasonably good look at was the island of Hawai'i—and he, like most of his compatriots, was greatly impressed by what he called "by far the worst part of the

island . . . as barren waste looking a country as can be conceived to exist in the Neighborhood of a fine one." King estimated the size of this apparently lava covered and "barren" district known as Ka'ū, the coast of which, he said, "presents a prospect of the most horrid and dreary kind," as bounding "half of the SE beech, & all the s neck"—in other words, about a fifth to a quarter of the island's coastline.[38] In later reducing his original all-island population estimate from 500,000 to 400,000, King seems to have incorporated this observation into a rough rule of thumb, not knowing, of course, that (with the exception of Haleakalā on Maui) the island of Hawai'i was unique in having active volcanoes and thus also was alone in possessing in large areas the land conditions that he saw at Ka'ū. On the other major islands the coastal population was so dense that even the worst areas for habitation were thoroughly populated—on O'ahu, for instance, the harsh and dry limestone area around Kalaeloa (Barber's Point) in the 'Ewa district, where pre-1778 access to the freshwater lens was obtained through sinkholes and wells.[39]

Indeed, even the area on the island of Hawai'i that so impressed King with its barrenness was in fact well populated. Fresh water springs bubble up all along the coastline and archaeological evidence—including the existence to this day of a number of very large man-made fishponds—points to intensive pre-*haole* coastal habitation.[40] Cook described "a pritty large village" at the southernmost point in the district, "the inhabitants of which thronged off to the ship with hogs and women."[41] For that matter, King himself noted in his journal that "horrid & dismal as this part of the Island appears, yet there are many villages interspersed . . . [and] there are houses built even on the ruins we have described." Moreover, he added: "Fishing is a principal occupation with the Inhabitants, which they sold to us, & we also had a very plentiful supply of other food when off this s end."[42] But, years later, as he reconsidered his first impressions and reduced his population estimate down to 400,000, it seems that all he remembered was that "horrid & dismal" appearing coastline. Today, however, there is no excuse for accepting his greatly erroneous assumption that a quarter of the all-island coastline was uninhabited.

An additional point should be made here. There is a long-standing ethological and anthropological environmental precept used by scholars that has been called "Romer's Rule." It postulates that "both human and nonhuman groups tend to be conservative in their development, simply changing in an attempt to maintain the status quo intact in a changing environment." Anthropologist Catherine Hodge McCoid (formerly Masering) has proposed an application of Romer's Rule to explain certain observed demographic phenomena throughout the world: "populations tend to expand first into areas with climates most like those of their own area."[43] McCoid's hypothesis joins both observation and common sense in Hawai'i: in every case the lush windward sides of the islands were settled first, with expansion into the drier areas generally occurring only when the densities of the windward areas were sufficient to require such expansion. The repeated evidence of substantial (but relatively late-settled) pre-*haole* Hawaiian communities in the harshest environments on all the Hawaiian islands means that the more hospitable environments must long before have been filled to capacity. And, as we shall soon see, the carrying capacities of those environments were enormous.

4. Finally, there is what in fact was King's first incorrect assumption, that "the interior parts of the country are entirely uninhabited." In addition to ample archaeological evidence of inland populations throughout the islands, the traditional *mauka/ makai* (mountain/sea) economic arrangements of the Hawaiians required substantial inland populations in a number of areas.[44] But one historical example is particularly striking, and again provides an insight to help explain King's thinking. On January 6, 1779, Cook sent then Master Bligh ashore near the southernmost tip of the island of Hawai'i. Upon his return to the ship Bligh reported that no fresh water was available "and that the surface of the Country was wholy composed of large slags and ashes here and there partly covered with plants."[45] They made sail and moved on. What neither Bligh nor Cook—nor King—knew, however, was what would have greeted them had they pushed about ten miles inland from the South Point coast. They would have found "the fertile valleys and lush uplands of this region, thickly populated and well cultivated" with "the most enchanting scenes of rural industry" that the surgeon and naturalist Archibald Menzies

discovered on his inland trip to that area sixteen years later and that would be destroyed by volcanic eruption only late in the 19th century:

> When we stopped in the evening we were surrounded by such a concourse of people who pressed so close to us that we could scarcely stir. . . . The economy with which these people laid out and managed their ground and the neatness with which they cultivated their little fields made the whole valley appear more like a rich garden than a plantation. A stream of water which fell from the mountain through the middle of it was ingeniously branched off on each side to flood and fertilize the most distant fields at pleasure.[46]

Then later, at another inland site—again in the district that from shipboard appeared so "barren and waste looking":

> We found the people everywhere busily employed in their little fields, many of which were here cropped with plantains and bananas that had a ragged appearance from having little or no shelter, yet they bore fruit tolerably well. . . . We observed here that they suffer many of their fields here and there to lay fallow, and these in general were cropped with fine grass, which they cut down for the purpose of covering their new planted fields of taro or yams to preserve them from the powerful heat of the sun.[47]

We are even fortunate enough to have a visual record of one of the smaller inland villages visited by Menzies near the large Kapāpala plantation and thought by King to be non-existent: the well-known drawing by Thomas Heddington, "Village of Macacoupah, Owhyee," [Figure 2] done about eight miles in from the coast of Ka'ū while the artist was waiting for Menzies to return from his trek up the side of Mauna Loa, clearly shows in the background acre upon acre of carefully laid out and well cultivated agricultural fields.[48]

For many years now, it has been well known in other parts of the Pacific—for example, New Zealand (Aotearoa)—that the earliest Western explorers substantially underestimated indigenous populations by failing to consider numerous inland inhabitants. It seems about time that the same correction is made for Hawai'i. As archaeologists David Denison and Arthur Forman have concluded: "archaeological research of inland areas can be as rewarding as the more traditional work on the coastal areas in the under-

Figure 2. "Village of Macacoupah, Owhyee," by Thomas Heddington (1794), an intensely cultivated and well-populated inland village on the island of Hawai'i (Courtesy of Bishop Museum Photo Archives.)

standing of prehistoric Hawaiian culture. Indeed, comprehensive understanding *cannot* be gained without research in these areas."[49]

To sum up, all the evidence available to us regarding the credibility of King's 1778 population estimate points in precisely the opposite direction from that which most subsequent writers have alleged: King's 400,000 estimate was, if anything, a serious *under* estimate of the actual figure. But how far short was he? There are several techniques that can be employed in addressing this question, but before turning to them it is worth a brief look at what is suggested merely by what we have done so far.

—First, King's estimate of the permanent population at Kealakekua Bay appears to have been a bare minimum, and possibly a serious understatement, of the actual numbers. In addition to the fact that other contemporary estimates were higher, the presence of later estimates showing only a relatively slight reduction in the area's population—compared with an all-island rate of loss at least three or four times as high, even using what we shall soon see is a greatly understated depopulation rate—suggest that King's estimate of the Kealakekua Bay population probably fell significantly short of reality.

Even if King's Kealakekua Bay estimate had been correct—and all his other incorrect assumptions correct as well—the actual coastal mileage of the islands known to have been inhabited projects out to an all-island population of 478,000, not the 400,000 he thought.[50] If Samwell's slightly larger house count at Kealakekua Bay is substituted for King's (and, again, all King's other dubious assumptions are accepted), the all-island projection reaches nearly 515,000. Note, too, that we are not considering here the possibility that King also may have underestimated the number of residents per house—something that by itself could have an enormous impact on an upward revision of his figures. For example, even if all King's other assumptions were correct, but there were an average of eight people per household (as the *Missionary Herald* later reported during a time when average household size was substantially smaller than in 1778–79, due to the devastating effects of venereal disease on the birthrate) and not King's "very moderate allowance" of six, King's all-island population extrapolation would have approached 640,000.

Further, if instead of the greatly varied King/Samwell/Ledyard house counts we accept the 1822 population count for Kealakekua Bay and assume it to have suffered a depopulation rate between 1778 and 1822 that is consistent with just the *lowest* possible all-island depopulation rate, we arrive at a 1778 Kealakekua Bay population per coastal mile of just over 1100 people.[51] This only means an upward revision of the Bay's total population from King's 2400 to 3300. However, projecting this out (with all of King's other unrealistically limiting assumptions intact, including the guess that 25 percent of the coastline was uninhabited and the belief that no one lived inland) we achieve an all-island figure of 658,000 people.

—The second point discussed above concerned King's assumption that the population density at Kealakekua Bay was consistent along the entire coastline of the island of Hawai'i and throughout all the other populated islands as well. As we have seen, this assumption was incorrect. This is so, first, because the windward coast of the island of Hawai'i (and of all the other islands) was much more heavily populated—as water, soil, and political conditions dictated, as other observers noted, and as is almost invariably the case with island populations; and, second, because the older islands of Maui, Kaua'i, and O'ahu—especially O'ahu— were proportionately much more fertile and much more densely populated than was the island of Hawai'i. King's error here is no doubt traceable to the fact that Cook's ships failed to come in contact with or even draw close to what are now known to have been the most thickly populated parts of the various islands. The mistake on King's part, in itself, provides no clue as to how far upward his estimate should be revised, but it does clearly show that whatever minimal all-island projection is made from the Kealakekua Bay population—a corrected projection ranging from 478,000 to 658,000 (putting Ledyard's much larger house count aside)—it is far too small.

—The third of King's assumptions that we examined was his stipulation that a quarter of the total all-island coastline was uninhabited. We saw that this assumption, though an understandable error, was a gross exaggeration. Again, we have no way of numerically correcting the mistake with any sense of confidence. However, in view of the fact that even the most inhospitable coastal areas were well populated on all the islands—from the steep, rough, and arid western coastline of Lāna'i to the lava covered areas of the least densely-settled major island of Hawai'i—it is unlikely that any but the smallest fraction of the all-island coastline was uninhabited. Although it too is probably a greatly excessive guess, a figure of ten percent would seem much closer to the actual pre-*haole* situation. The effect of this no doubt conservative adjustment (and, once again, ignoring for the moment the clearly incorrect assumptions regarding the representativeness of Kealakekua Bay's population density and the matter of inland population) results in a lifting of the minimum all-island population projection from the 478,000–658,000 range to a range of from 574,000 to more than 789,000.

—Finally, the fourth key assumption of King's that we looked at was his belief that the islands contained no inland population at all. We saw that both archaeological and historical evidence show this assumption to be incorrect; indeed, in some areas the inland population density no doubt greatly exceeded that of certain less desirable coastal areas. Again, unfortunately, we have no way of numerically estimating the size of the overall inland population. However, even if it only amounted to ten percent of the total population (a dubiously low estimate, perhaps, in view of the vigorous traditional exchange patterns between coastal and inland peoples in certain locales) the all-island population projection ascends to a range of between 635,000 to 875,000—and still we have not factored in the second, and probably most important, of King's mistaken assumptions, that the Kealakekua Bay density was consistent, for both leeward and windward areas, throughout all the inhabited islands. Any minimal adjustment for this error—for example, assuming a 3 to 2 windward/leeward density ratio to account for military parity (probably a major underestimate of the windward population in light of the long-term 10 to 1 or 15 to 1 ratio of irrigated taro to dry-land taro production potential) and conservatively projecting the overall density of the island of Hawai'i onto the other, more thickly-settled islands—easily pushes the higher estimate range from 800,000 to well over one million. And we are still dealing, at each stage of adjustment, with only the *low* end of each possible correction.

It is possible, of course, that despite the caution exerted at each stage of this reconsideration of King's assumptions, one or more of these corrections may be an overstatement. For example, on some islands there is as yet little archaeological evidence of a significant inland population; it is thus possible that 10 percent is too high an estimate of the total population living inland—although, either way, this figure is hardly more than a guess and it is equally possible that 10 percent is too low. (Most inland areas have never been closely studied by archaeologists and with every passing year major new inland settlements and agricultural terraces—such as, most recently, Luluku on O'ahu—are rediscovered.) In any case, the extremely conservative nature of each individual adjustment—particularly regarding the crucial matter of windward/leeward population density ratios—leaves ample room for error in all cases without reducing the overall estimate to less than 800,000. This is so, in fact, even if there were no inland population at all on any of the islands.

Now, clearly, numbers of this magnitude will seem absurd to those for whom Schmitt's 200,000 to 300,000 or even King's 400,000 have become truisms. (The same initial reaction greeted the much more drastic upward revisions of the pre-Columbian population estimates of the Americas.) Yet, these new estimates derive, it must be repeated, merely from a *conservative* critique of what is by far the best contemporary estimate of the 1778 population. While it is true that any estimate of the entire archipelago's population based on extrapolation from a first-hand count of a single small area is fraught with risk, it is in fact the procedure that has undergirded every previous estimate from King to Schmitt. Given the limited data available, it is unavoidable that any estimate begin with King—and the discussion of King that has just followed is, by far, the most detailed such analysis ever attempted. Still, whereas even the best previous estimates have stopped with a critical examination of King's work, I propose that we now test the possibility that the pre-*haole* population may have reached 800,000 or more by asking three crucial questions about this new range of estimates: 1) Is it possible for the population to have grown to such size from the time of the first tiny Polynesian settlements? 2) Can the Hawaiian islands have fed and otherwise supported this many people? 3) What happened to the people—is there anything that credibly can be said to have reduced such a seemingly enormous native population down to barely 40,000 by the early 1890s? These are the questions we will address in the following pages.

II

Growth, Sustenance, and Collapse

Hawai'i was one of the last areas in Polynesia to have been settled by humans, and it is generally believed that there was little or no in-migration between the time of the first settlements and a possible small in-migration from Tahiti around the 12th century A.D. Since it is often assumed that the first settlers numbered, at most, in only the low to mid-hundreds, is it possible for a population of 800,000 or 1,000,000—or even more—to have been attained by 1778?

We necessarily will be dealing here with a good bit of conjecture and will be relying upon comparisons with other populations to construct something of a model. To begin, however, we should note that it is now known that the first human settlers arrived in Hawai'i at least as early as the first century A.D. As with all archaeological dating, we probably never will discover the earliest sites of human habitation, but recent radiocarbon datings from both windward and leeward O'ahu show settlement there between the third century B.C. and the first century A.D. We also know, from the evidence of items the early settlers brought with them, as well as from computer simulations of Pacific wind and current patterns, that they came in a deliberate settlement effort, not merely on drift voyages.[1]

The matter of deliberate settlement is important because it indicates that there would have been a reasonably balanced sex ratio among the earliest settlers. After all, the Polynesians certainly knew as well as anyone else that a successful settlement would require a sufficient number of women to give rise to succeeding generations. Thus, as we attempt to reconstruct a population growth picture of pre-*haole* Hawai'i, we can begin with two basic assumptions: sometime at least as early as the beginning of the second century A.D. there was in Hawai'i a deliberate human settlement—and that settlement most likely had a sex ratio favorable to reproduction.

How large was the settlement? It is conventionally assumed, as I have noted, to have numbered no more than in the low to middle hundreds (though it may have been larger and may have been smaller) so a reasonably conservative guess would be one hundred, with a fairly equal balance of males and females. (Some twin-hulled Polynesian voyaging canoes were capable of carrying 80 to 100 persons and of remaining at sea for four to six weeks; even centuries after they had given up long-distance open-sea voyaging, the Hawaiians sailed canoes holding as many as sixty or seventy people.)[2] How rapidly might such a small population have grown and what size might it have attained by 1778? Here we must turn to some statistical probabilities based on the experiences of other peoples and then to computer simulations of population growth on Pacific islands in general.

For many years demographers have attempted to estimate the minimum size an isolated population must begin with in order for it to survive and grow. It is now clear, however, that specific conditions are more important than raw numbers and it has been demonstrated that under favorable conditions a founding group of only six people can readily establish a viable and expanding population. To do so, however, would seem to require an extremely rapid early growth rate. Thus, archaeologist Patrick Kirch recently has said that "there is no reason to suppose that growth rates among colonizing prehistoric Polynesians were appreciably lower than that of Pitcairn." Pitcairn, of course, is the island settled by the *Bounty* mutineers and their Tahitian wives, a group that, early on at least, apparently doubled in size approximately each generation, for an intrinsic growth rate of about 4.0 percent annually.[3]

A growth rate this high, which today is characteristic only of places like Kenya and, to a somewhat lesser extent, Nigeria, Iran, Pakistan, Bangladesh, and parts of Latin America—with birth rates more than eight times the death rate—would be impossible to sustain indefinitely. Suppose, then, that after just two centuries of such Pitcairn-like expansion, the growth rate of our model second century Hawaiian settler group of 100 people dropped suddenly to conform with the characteristics of a United Nations population model designed to describe "an agricultural population with high birth rates and mortality somewhat lower than primitive levels." This model—which produces an annual growth rate of 1.23 percent and a doubling time of 57 years—assumes, for example, a life expectancy of 30 years (combined for both sexes) and an infant mortality rate of 264.9 per 1000 births (meaning that more than one out of every four infants born dies before its first birthday).[4] As will be discussed later, there is very good reason to believe that such assumptions are too harsh to properly describe pre-*haole* Hawaiian society (which, as we shall see, appears to have had an exceptionally low infant mortality rate), but I am trying to be conservative. Finally, let us suppose that there was no further in-migration until Captain Cook's arrival in 1778. What size population would a growth rate based on these assumptions produce in Hawai'i by 1778?

Such a model would produce a population equalling Schmitt's 1778 estimate of 200,000 to 300,000 by the late fifth or early sixth centuries; by the latter part of the seventh century such a growth rate would already have pushed the population past 3 million—and past 100 million before the close of the tenth century, or about double the population of tenth century China! Surely, this will not do. But the example at least suggests the potential power of population growth dynamics.

A much more precise set of models appropriate to early population growth on Pacific islands was developed about a decade ago. Three Australian scholars—Norma McArthur, I. W. Saunders, and R. L. Tweedie—very carefully constructed a series of computer simulations of possible growth rates among small and isolated Pacific island populations. Building into each simulation a host of demographic variables (ages of individuals at time of settlement, fertility and mortality rates, marital age restrictions, sex ratios, incest prohibitions, and so on—based on historical evidence of Pacific peoples) they entered into the computer details on each imagined individual originally in or subsequently born into the population. "At the end of each 'year,' " as they put it, "the computer performs a 4-stage operation: it creates the year's births, deaths and marriages within the population present at the start of the 'year' and then adds one year to the ages of those who survived to its end, thus generating the population 'at risk' for the following 'year,' when the same sequence of operations is performed."[5]

The various populations modeled in the study's simulations fell into three categories that McArthur, Saunders, and Tweedie labeled "presumed successes," "doubtfuls," and "headed for extinction"—depending on how the myriad combination of factors worked out in their individual computer runs. Of the "presumed successes" (the only category that matters here since the actual Hawaiian settlement was a success) they reported that "more than 90 percent had average growth rates within the range of 0.50 to 1.49 percent per year, with more than half within the range of 0.75 to 1.24 percent."[6] Overall, the intrinsic growth rate implied in the "Pacific model" was 1.78 percent per year; and, of the successful examples on which details were provided, the lowest growth rate was attained by a group labeled "C" which had an effective 0.9 percent per annum growth rate over the course of three hundred years. (The simulation ended at that point.) The highest of the three plotted growth rate simulations was well over 2.0 percent annually.[7]

For various reasons, then, a growth rate of 0.9 percent per annum for the first 300 years of the initial Hawaiian settlement (less than one-fourth the early Pitcairn growth rate) would seem extremely conservative. In addition to the fact that it is the lowest growth rate of the successful populations for which McArthur, Saunders, and Tweedie plotted a detailed evolutionary course, some of the specifications built into the model are unrealistically restrictive for application to the actual Hawaiian settlement. For example, the 0.9 percent growth simulation is based on a founding population of only six people, thus greatly magnifying any negative factors such as individual infertility or subfecundity or a premature accidental death of one of the women. It also assumes that child-bearing is restricted to "married" women, that monogamous sexual restraints are in effect, and that the combined life expectancy of males and females is only 27 years—none of which probably prevailed in the Hawaiian case.

Moreover, whereas this relatively low-growth initial population is still proportionately ascending after 300 years in the McArthur, Saunders, and Tweedie model, I propose that we cap the 0.9 percent growth at that point and drop the subsequent growth rate to 0.52 percent per annum. This is a growth rate that results in a population doubling time of less than once in every six generations. That is 20 percent lower than the growth rate suggested by Hawaiian archaeological remains throughout the pre-*haole* period, as archaeologist Robert Hommon has shown. It barely falls into the "presumed success" range of the McArthur, Saunders, and Tweedie simulations. It is the figure used by anthropologist/demographer Fekri A. Hassan as a reasonable growth rate among prehistoric peoples practicing a prolonged (and in our case unrealistic) 40-month period of child-spacing and living in environments much less benign than that of Hawai'i. And it is even well below the growth rate of 0.63 percent per annum assumed by Robert Schmitt himself in constructing a projected population growth curve for Hawai'i since the date of first settlement—a date that at the time of the curve's construction he thought to be somewhere around 500 A.D. (It is worth noting, by the way, that, when corrected for date of first settlement, this population projection of Schmitt's results in a 1778 population of well over one and a half million.)[8]

To get a better sense of how modest our posited growth rate of 0.52 percent per annum is—in Hawai'i's extremely healthful environment—it is about the same as the growth rate achieved in England under the most wretched conditions between the early 15th and early 17th centuries, two hundred years framed on each end by the worst bubonic plague epidemics in English history, two hundred years themselves marked by widespread starvation and (in addition to recurrent plague epidemics that convulsed London and the countryside at least once every two or three decades) two hundred years of constant pestilential devastation from typhus, smallpox, syphilis, dysentery, and more—none of which existed in Hawai'i. Our proposed growth rate for Hawai'i is even, in fact, about 50 percent lower than that experienced by Ireland during the disastrous century that ended just after the great potato blight—an Ireland so destitute, diseased, and hungry before the blight that, out of a maximum attained population of about 8 million, nearly 2 million people left for England, Scotland, and America; an Ireland so devastated by the blight itself that an additional million people emigrated while a million and half died of starvation and disease in just four years.[9]

Plotting this very modest overall growth pattern from the time of a founding settlement of 100 persons at the start of the second century A.D. (the very latest likely date of first settlement) results in a projected 7th century population of about 6400 people. This number fits well with archaeological findings that by the 7th century (and before) the population of Hawai'i had spread out from what appear to be the earliest settlements on the island of O'ahu to numerous sites from one end of the chain of major islands to the other—from fishing villages at the arid southern tip of the island of Hawai'i to (more than 300 miles away) agricultural villages possibly employing irrigation techniques on the lush northern side of the island of Kaua'i; from temporary (possibly hunting or religious) sites on the floor of Haleakalā crater on the island of Maui (a climb of about 10,000 feet) to permanent settlements in Hālawa Valley on the island of Moloka'i.[10]

By the end of the 17th century, nearly a hundred years before the arrival of Captain Cook, this same greatly restrained rate of expansion—with no allowance for in-migration since the time of initial settlement—would have produced a population well in excess of 800 thousand people. By 1778 it would have been closing in on one and a half million. Any marked in-migration around the 12th century (to say nothing of adjustments for the unrealistic inhibitions built into the models themselves) would have the effect of pushing the 1778 population well over 2 million.

Now, I am not claiming that the population of Hawai'i ever was this high. I merely am saying—in answer to the first question posed earlier—that the dynamics of even the most conservative population growth models are such that the population easily *could* have grown to, say, a million or more were the environment able to sustain such growth. Indeed, if the Hawaiian population in 1778 was "only" between 800,000 and 1,000,000, the serious historical growth rate question that needs to be addressed is: What kept it so low? We will discuss later some of the restraints that other writers have suggested may have been in force.

But, it will certainly be protested, even if the small settler groups in theory could have grown to such previously unsuspected size, could the *resources* of the islands have supported such large numbers? Merely to ask this question is to enter one of the most complex and intensely contested current debates among archaeologists, demographers, and others. The phrase "carrying capacity" is at the center of that debate and, as one anthropologist has recently pointed out, the term itself has come to involve such a "bewildering variety of definitions and formulae for its calculation" that some anthropologists have decided to abandon the concept altogether, while, conversely, others more and more see it as the key to a future new understanding of ecological analysis.[11]

To work out a reasonably thorough estimate of the carrying capacity of the Hawaiian islands would require detailed analyses of climates and micro-climates, soil conditions on all the islands and on the different parts of individual islands, levels of agricultural sophistication, specific crops grown and their yields under the varied prevailing conditions, other foodstuff availability (such as fish and wildlife), caloric requirements per person—and a good deal more. And still, controversy would be inevitable.

It is not my intention to conduct such an analysis. Instead, all I am seeking to determine is whether the carrying capacity of pre-*haole* Hawai'i—whatever it may have been specifically—was sufficient to support comfortably a population of three to four times the current prevailing estimates of that population. A population of 800,000 in pre-*haole* Hawai'i, for example, would have meant a population density of about 124 people per square mile—or, if 90 percent of the population lived along the coastline, 903 people per coastal mile. A population of one million would have meant 155 people per square mile or 1129 per coastal mile, again, if 90 percent of the population were concentrated in coastal areas. Are either of these sets of numbers within the realm of possibility? Let us look at two very different kinds of non-industrial communities, on opposite sides of the Pacific Ocean, for some comparative information.

The coast of Peru extends more than 1700 miles from southern Equador to northern Chile. It is an extremely inhospitable area for human habitation, and agriculture in particular is an exceptionally difficult way of life. Rainfall is light to non-existent and the population that developed along the coastline prior to European contact nourished itself primarily on ocean resources. Indeed, when agriculture did begin to develop, the emphasis was on cotton and gourds—two non-food crops that were used to support fishing endeavors.[12] In time another form of agriculture emerged and became fairly widespread, sunken field agriculture. As one historian describes it:

> With no measurable rainfall and no major source of irrigation, crops were grown in depressions that were close enough to the water table to provide moisture for plant roots. When maize was planted in the Chilca sunken fields, a small fish was deposited with the kernel in order to provide fertilizer and perhaps moisture during germination.[13]

Under these harsh conditions the coastal population of Peru grew to a conservatively estimated peak of 6.5 million people by the time of Western contact—that is, over 3800 people per coastal mile.[14] A similar population per coastal mile in Hawai'i—which, of course, had a vastly superior living situation—would produce a total population in excess of 3 million people.

From the coast of Peru, turning to the Highlands of New Guinea is an instructive contrast. Not contacted by the outside world until barely 50 years ago, the isolated Highland peoples do not, of course, have any ocean resources available to them. Instead, they practice intense sweet potato cultivation as their main source of nourishment, although "mixed garden" plantings (taro, yams, bananas, and other crops) supplement the diets in specific areas. In addition, wild pigs are hunted and domestic pigs are raised for feasts—but pig is not a commonplace dietary item anywhere in New Guinea. A good deal of anthropological research has been conducted in the Highlands and it has been found that areas containing 50 to 100 people per square mile are common enough to be considered "moderate" in terms of population density, and densities among specific peoples are often vastly higher—more than 400 per square mile among the Dugum Dani, well over 500 per square mile among the Tsembaga, and nearly 750 per square mile among the Naregu Chimbu, for example. To be sure, these densities do not prevail throughout the Highlands, but even at these higher numbers it is estimated that the most densely populated communities are living at barely half to two-thirds of their maximum potential densities.[15]

Peru and New Guinea are far from unusual. Many other examples could be cited, including the Maya of the Yucatan Lowlands who, more than a thousand years ago, attained population densities ranging in places from nearly 600 persons per square mile to over 5000 per square mile. Even today Yucatan cultivators, now reduced to shifting swidden agriculture, maintain densities of well over 200 people per square mile.[16] With these figures in mind, recall that a population of one million in Hawai'i would have produced a density of only 155 people per square mile.

Coastal Peru and the New Guinea Highlands and the Lowlands of the Yucatan, for all their differences, are similar in one small respect: all of them are almost totally dependent on the resources of either the land or the sea; none of them has what Hawai'i does —rich and fertile land *and* ocean resources. This environmental situation—what some British archaeologists call the "double larder" phenomenon because of the extensive nutritional support of both environments—can permit enormous population densities in island settings. Thus, for example, the huge Caribbean island of Hispaniola—29,500 square miles—had an estimated 8 million (and possibly many more) inhabitants prior to contact with the West, a density of 271 people per square mile. On the other end of the geographic scale, tiny Tapituea (Drummond's Island) in Polynesia had in 1841 an estimated 10 thousand people packed into 20 square miles, a density of 500 per square mile; and Banaba (Ocean Island) has never been considered especially remarkable for the fact that in pre-*haole* times its nine square miles of coral land supported a permanent population of at least 2500 people, more than 275 per square mile. Other examples abound—ranging from some North-Central Polynesian Outlier atolls with densities of 300, 400, 700, and even 1500 people per square mile (some of which are densities only half their estimated pre-*haole* carrying capacities) to a number of other islands in Micronesia with densities in excess of 1000 and 2000 people per square mile.[17]

This is not to suggest that Hawai'i ever had densities even approaching this higher range. But it is worth noting that even in the 19th century, when Hawaiian agricultural skills were far less than what they had been in pre-*haole* times, missionaries on all the islands estimated that dry-land taro fields could feed from two to four persons per acre (1300 to 2600 per cultivated square mile) and wet-land taro could sustain populations of between 15 and 30 persons per acre (10,000 to 20,000 per cultivated square mile).[18] What this means is that—not even considering the other half of the "double larder," the resources of the sea—pre-*haole* Hawai'i easily could have fed over a million people with less than two percent of the land being put into combined dry-land and wet-land taro production. In short, it does not stretch the imagination a bit to suggest that in pre-*haole* times Hawai'i attained a probable population density at least in the 125 to 150 people per square mile range.

To get another sense of how modest such a density projection is for Hawai'i, a comparison with late 14th century England is instructive. Throughout the 13th century major climatic changes had been occurring in the northern hemisphere that reached a peak in the first half of the 14th century. Storms of exceptional violence pounded the coastlines and entire English towns and villages were washed away. Glaciers extended further south during this time than they had in over a thousand years, while heavily traveled sailing routes in the North Atlantic Ocean and the Norwegian Sea became blocked by ice. The Thames and other rivers froze for weeks and months at a time; when not frozen they frequently overflowed their banks causing terrible floods; at still other times, in summer, they almost dried up. For decades on end fishing became an almost impossible profession—and this was long before, even in the best of times, large amounts of cod or even salted and preserved herring were available. Harvest failures were common and, as historian Fernand Braudel has pointed out, during these times throughout Europe "one bad harvest was just about bearable; if there were two, prices went mad and famine set in." In fact, England was wracked by devastating famines from 1315 to 1317; less cataclysmic starvation times were routine. Moreover, whether or not the harvest failed in a particular year, England's already primitive agricultural yields dropped by an estimated 16 percent during the first half of the 14th century. The economy was collapsing. The population—already more thinly distributed by far than any of the major countries in Europe—was declining as well.[19]

To all this there was then added the *coup de grace,* the worst bacteriological invasion in all the history of Europe; at mid-century the Black Death devastated England, killing at least a third and possibly close to half the already small and declining population. Other plague outbreaks followed in 1361, 1368, 1369, 1371, and 1375. In the aftermath of the great pestilence literally thousands of rural settlements became ghost towns, empty and abandoned. All over the country vast cultivated fields were reclaimed by forests and meadows. A conservative estimate of England's population density in the wake of all this, for the year 1377, is about 52 people per square mile—barely the density attained in ancient Sumer 4500 years ago. As French historian Georges Duby has shown, however, such medieval population estimates are invariably far too low. Based solely on the number of financially solvent households liable for taxation, such estimates consistently fail to count those (apparently a good many) who falsified their finances to avoid a levy, as well as the great multitudes of the genuinely destitute. Still—counting only those relative few who appear in the fiscal records, in the wake of the worst disaster in the history of the most sparsely populated country in Europe at the time—the lowest possible population density for the half-deserted hell-hole that was England in 1377 would have meant in Hawai'i a population of over 335,000 people. If an accurate census were used for England at this time of desolation, the equivalent population density for Hawai'i would result in a total population well in excess of 600,000 to 700,000. There should be little doubt that the comparatively paradisiacal environment of Hawai'i—with its exceptionally robust and nearly disease-free people having reaped for nearly two millennia the huge harvests of both the land and the sea—would have supported a population a great deal larger than that.[20]

But we need not look to late medieval England, or pre-Columbian Peru, or the Highlands of New Guinea, or the Yucatan of a thousand years ago, or the Caribbean island of Hispaniola, or the islands and atolls of Micronesia for our carrying capacity comparisons. In fact, a Hawaiian population density of 130 to 150 per square mile (which would mean a total population ranging from just under 840,000 to nearly a million) would be comfortably in the low-middle range of the probable densities of Tahiti and the Marquesas, Hawai'i's closest island cousins on the eve of Western contact, as well as harsh and dry pre-*haole* Rapanui (Easter Island) and the Mangarevas—all in Eastern Polynesia and all possessing pre-*haole* population densities ranging from well over 100 persons per square mile to more than 1000 persons per square mile.[21]

Finally, readers familiar with present-day Hawai'i may protest that a total pre-*haole* population in the range that I am suggesting is nearly as large as Hawai'i's population today. As one reader of a draft of this piece commented, this "may strike some intuitively as unreasonable." Such readers need to be reminded, however, that—in addition to the absence in ancient Hawai'i of today's cars, trucks, hotels, shopping centers, airports, warehouses, freeways, and the other steel and concrete accoutrements of industrial life—the population of pre-*haole* Hawaii was much more equitably distributed than it is today. A roughly balanced all-island population distribution of more than 800,000 people would amount to a density approximately the same as that currently existing on the eastern half of the rural island of Kaua'i *without* the population of the town of Līhu'e, the second largest town on the island. It also is about the same as the densities, on O'ahu, of the Waialua and Ko'olauloa districts—the sparsely settled northern half of the island from Kualoa all the way up and around to Mākaha, including no large towns and vast uninhabited open spaces in the middle of the island and even along much of the coastline. These are far from crowded conditions, but they produce a population density of over 130 persons per square mile.

To be sure, the populations of some islands—particularly O'ahu—were more densely concentrated than this, while others—particularly Hawai'i—were less densely inhabited. And, as we have seen, the windward sides of all the islands were more densely settled than the leeward sides. In addition, many areas of the islands that today are deserted, remote, and even inaccessible except by helicopter—from the deep valleys between north Kohala and Hāmākua on the north shore of Hawai'i to the Nā Pali cliffs and valleys of Kaua'i—were heavily populated in pre-*haole* times as is evidenced both by the testimony of the earliest Western visitors to Hawai'i and by the impressive agricultural and habitation terraces, particularly in the Nā Pali area, that were constructed in the 12th century and before, the extensive ruins of which remain in place to this day.[22] [See Figure 3] But the point simply is that in pre-*haole* times there was nothing like the extreme population imbalance that presently exists in Hawai'i, the imbalance that gives rise to the false intuitive *impression* that pre-*haole* population size could not have attained today's magnitude.

Figure 3. Nu'ulolo'āina, Nā Pali on Kaua'i, terraces going down the valley—an example of pre-*haole* terraced agriculture on sloping land in a now-deserted and almost inaccessible area. (Courtesy of Bishop Museum Department of Anthropology.)

In sum, all the data plainly show that there can be no doubt concerning the second of the three questions asked earlier: whether it actually did or did not, Hawai'i was clearly *capable* of sustaining a population many times the conventionally estimated figure of 200,000 to 300,000, many times even King's estimates of 400,000 and 500,000. All that is required to accept this assertion is a willingness to believe that the Hawaiians possessed the same levels of agricultural and fishing competence as other Polynesians. These were, after all, the people commonly called by early visitors (to cite one) "the most industrious people I ever saw"; they were people who were such "dexterous fishers," noted another representative observer, that a day's outing in a given area would routinely result in "ten or twelve canoes deeply loaded," some dragging nets too full to lift on board; they were people who, alone among Pacific island societies, developed sophisticated aquaculture farms that produced additional thousands of tons of fish each year; they were people who just as expertly farmed land—tens of thousands of acres—of which it was said "nothing in nature can be more abundantly prolific," people whose "indefatigable labor" in cultivating and irrigating that land, wrote still another observer, "surpassed anything of the kind we had ever seen before."[23] To repeat, all it takes to believe that the ancient Hawaiians could have maintained and supported a population as large as that existing in Hawai'i today is a recognition that these extraordinarily inventive and assiduous people were capable of feeding a population with an attained density that was common among their Pacific island neighbors.

A small settlement in the first century A.D. easily, then, could have grown to well over a million people by the time of Western contact—and the Hawaiian Islands easily could have supported a native population of that size and more. But, just a hundred years after European contact, the native population of Hawai'i had fallen to less than 48,000. By the 1890s it was under 40,000. That implies a 4 or 5 to 1 depopulation ratio over the course of a century if Schmitt's 1778 estimate is correct or a more than 8 to 1 depopulation ratio if King's 400,000 figure is correct. An 8 to 1 depopulation ratio means that for every 800 Hawaiians alive in 1778 only 100 were alive in 1878. This is a population collapse vastly more destructive than the one suffered by medieval Europeans at the hands of the Black Death. Is it reasonable to believe that such horrifying figures, brought on primarily by imported disease, could actually be an *under* estimate?

It is known, from the first credible missionary census, that the native population of Hawai'i was about 130,000 in the year 1832, and probably at least a few thousand more in 1828—50 years after Western contact. By 1878—another 50 years later—that population (including almost 3,500 part-Hawaiians) was officially listed at 47,508.²⁴ Thus (and on this there is no disagreement), in roughly the second half-century following European contact, the disease-riddled Hawaiian population declined by almost two-thirds—to be more precise, by a ratio of about 2.8 to 1. In contrast, if Schmitt's 1778 population estimate were correct, the depopulation ratio for roughly the *first* half century after Western contact was "only" somewhere between 1.5 and 1.9 to 1. If King's estimate were correct, the depopulation ratio for the same years was about 3 to 1—substantially higher than Schmitt's figure, but not much more than the 1828–1878 decline ratio.

Put in other terms, if King's estimate for 1778 were correct, the Hawaiian population would have declined by about 66.5 percent 50 years after contact, and by 88.1 percent after a century of contact. If Schmitt's estimate for 1778 is correct, the decline was about 40.8 percent after 50 years of contact, and 78.8 percent after a century of contact (using the mid-point of Schmitt's 1778 estimate range). Which, if either, set of figures is most likely to be correct? Could both of them, terrible as they are, be too low?

Here, again, the best recourse is to turn to comparative data. And there is a wealth of it, much more than can be surveyed here. It all, however, heads toward the same conclusion.

Consider, as a first example—because it was contacted first—the case of Hispaniola. As pointed out earlier in my discussion of carrying capacity, the best modern estimate of Hispaniola's population in 1492 is about 8 million. By 1535—well under half a century later—the native population was extinct.²⁵ Eight million people had disappeared, primarily from newly-introduced diseases.

Or consider another population mentioned earlier—that of ancient Peru. Prior to Western contact Peru's population stood at about 9 million, with about 6.5 million people residing along the coast. Within the first fifty years following Western contact, observes historian Noble David Cook:

> The population fell to slightly over 1 million [about an 88 percent collapse] and by 1620 stood at about 600,000. The overall decline was approximately 93 percent for the century following contact between the European and Andean inhabitant. *The collapse along Peru's coast was total.*²⁶

Nearly 8 and a half million people disappeared—again, primarily from introduced disease. Such stories are repeated again and again and again in the annals of Western contact with indigenous peoples. To note only a few examples among many:

—In the Cuchumatan Highlands of Guatemala the population fell by 82 percent in the first half century following European contact, by 94 percent after 140 years.[27]

—Among the Cayapo people of South America the visit of a single, disease-infected missionary caused the death of more than 99 percent of the population in less than 25 years.[28]

—In California the Tolowa Indian population declined by 92 percent less than 50 years after Western contact, while for California as a whole the decline may have been as much as 98 percent in barely a century.[29]

—On the Baja peninsula the population fell by over 90 percent in 75 years, following an earlier plague that already had greatly reduced the native numbers.[30]

—In Western Nicaragua the indigenous population fell by over 99 percent within 60 years of Western contact.[31]

—In Brazil greater than a third of all the *tribes* extant at one time (more than 80 out of 230) were totally exterminated by imported disease in a period of 60 years. Even today, observes one prominent scholar, "time and again, tribes contacted during recent decades have rapidly been reduced to half, a quarter, or less of their original strength by the first onslaught of unknown diseases . . . despite the efforts of modern medicine."[32]

—In Florida the native population fell by 75 percent within 15 years following European contact and 95 percent or more in a century.[33]

—In Iceland more than a third of the population died within two years following the introduction of a foreign disease.[34]

—In the Saskatchewan Province of western Canada a single newly introduced disease (tuberculosis) killed almost 10 percent of an Indian population *each year* after Western contact, finally tapering into decline only after more than half the population was dead.[35]

—In New England imported disease virtually extinguished the Patuxet tribe in two years and cut the Massachusett tribe from about 24,000 people to 750 in less than two decades—a 97 percent collapse—and *then* they were hit by a smallpox epidemic. Throughout all of New England the native population fell from perhaps 144,000 to 8–10,000 in about 75 years—a decline of around 93 percent—and this occurred before the major Indian-colonist wars of 1675.[36]

—In central Mexico the population fell by almost 95 percent within 75 years after initial contact with Europeans.[37]

—On the island of Cozumel, off the eastern coast of Mexico, over 96 percent of the people had died less than 70 years after Western contact.[38]

—In southeastern Australia between 94 and 96 percent of the Aboriginal population died off in just over 60 years.[39]

—In New Zealand (Aotearoa) the Maori population dropped by about 60 percent in 70 years and more than 75 percent in a century—one early epidemic killing so many people so rapidly that the survivors could not bury the dead. It would have been much worse, but Aotearoa was relatively late in being colonized, so that both colonists and Maori benefitted from vaccination.[40]

—In the Marquesas the population fell by 90 percent in 65 years and by more than 96 percent in just over a century.[41]

—On the island of Aneityum in Vanuatu (formerly the New Hebrides) the population collapsed by over 90 percent in less than 70 years.[42]

—In the Austral Islands the population of Rapa was said to have dropped by over 90 percent in less than 20 years; but this is a serious underestimate because the initial population figure used was taken *after* an epidemic that had caused "much sickness and death in the island." The nearby islands of Tubuai and Raivavae lost, respectively, 70 percent of their people in 14 years and more than 96 percent in 15 years.[43]

—In Tahiti the population fell by about 75 percent in 25 years and between 86 and 89 percent in just over 60 years.[44]

—In Rarotonga of the Cook Islands the population fell by 50 percent in just 15 years and by 75 percent in less than 40 years.[45]

—Still further east in Polynesia the population of Easter Island fell by over 98 percent from the time of first contact with the West to the end of the 19th century and that of the Mangareva Islands by at least 88 percent.[46]

Disasters of this magnitude—and much worse—were the rule rather than the exception during the years of first contact between Europeans and indigenous peoples throughout the Pacific and the Americas. Although the causes of some of these catastrophes included a combination of disease, warfare, enslavement, or other factors, the overwhelming cause in every case and the sole cause in most was newly-introduced infection. Having been spared for the preceding centuries from the diseases that had ravaged Europe and Asia, the native peoples of these areas found themselves without immunities to those diseases when Western contact was made. Disaster was often immediate, not even waiting the 40 or 50 or 70 or 100 years we have been discussing. Thus, the horrendously sudden population collapses that occurred, for example, in 19th century New Caledonia and Pohnpei—as noted earlier—had their parallels nearly eight thousand miles away in North America when, for instance, a single influenza epidemic early in the 20th century killed off more than half the Ojibwa people in a part of northwest Ontario. Earlier, 98 percent of the Mandan Indians had succumbed to an introduced disease in just a matter of weeks.[47]

Indeed, so common were epidemic death rates of 50 percent and more *per epidemic*, that anthropologists and historians have now taken to plotting pre-European population estimates based on varying probable disease mortality scenaria. For example, anthropologist William A. Starna has based his estimates of 17th century Mohawk Indian population on a statistical table that plots the consequences of 5-year epidemic mortality rates of either 50, 60, or 70 percent following Western contact, these numbers being the most common he found in other comparable situations. Starna settles on "a death rate of somewhere between fifty and sixty percent" as most likely for just the half-decade between 1634 and 1639.[48]

What all this adds up to that is relevant to Hawai'i are two conclusions that have become working norms of scholars doing research in these other areas:

1. A standard overall depopulation ratio of at least 20 to 1, from the time of first contact to the levelling-off point—usually about a century after contact—can commonly be counted on. This would give a pre-*haole* population for Hawai'i of roughly 800,000 to 950,000, depending on whether the calculation is based on the population remaining a century after contact or at the time when it apparently bottomed out or reached what is called "nadir." However, the 20 to 1 ratio is now often thought of—even by its author—as being too small, in many cases by half. Moreover, these ratios are for coastal and inland populations combined. Coastal populations alone (as we saw with Peru) had much higher depopulation ratios, generally more than double the overall figure; 45 or 50 to 1 ratios in coastal areas—meaning a 98 to 99 percent rate of decline—were common.[49] And, however many people lived inland in Hawai'i, certainly most of the population was concentrated along the coastlines.

2. In almost every case studied, the highest rate of decline by far has occurred in the years immediately following first contact, as would be epidemiologically predicted. After a precipitous early drop, when newly introduced disease is raging unchecked in a so-called "virgin soil" or "islanded" population, the decline slowly levels out—finally hitting bottom when, on average, a population is about 5 percent of its former size, or 1 to 2 percent of its former size in coastal areas. Figure 4 plots the King and Schmitt depopulation trajectories against a low average for similar contact situations for which there are credible estimates, excluding situations so disastrous that they led to extinction. As is readily seen, Schmitt's scenario for Hawai'i is so at odds with this conservative pattern that it actually inverts it! Instead of a precipitous early decline, followed by a gradual levelling-out, Schmitt's projection describes a relatively slow early decline that increases suddenly, and inexplicably, as soon as missionaries started taking censuses. The only tenable explanation for this anomaly is that Schmitt's estimate of the size of the pre-*haole* population—and consequently, the decline rate between 1778 and 1831—is vastly understated.

In Hawai'i, there was no further Western contact, and thus no written record, for most of the crucial decade following the death of Cook and the departure of his ships. However, there is ample evidence of the population being riddled with disease when Western records resumed after 1786, and there is also ample evidence of severe depopulation during that time.[50] But we can only guess at the actual numbers.

Nevertheless, using the standard measures of depopulation that we have seen are common in first-contact settings with the West—including settings as comparable as possible to Hawai'i's—it is readily apparent that Hawai'i's pre-*haole* population could easily have been 800,000 to 1,000,000, and possibly a great deal more. This is at least double King's estimate and four to five times Schmitt's lower-middle range figures. The answer to our earlier question, then, is clear: it is indeed quite possible that 4 or 5 to 1, or even 8 to 1, rates of depopulation for the Hawaiian people between 1778 and 1878 are underestimates. And underestimates by an extremely large margin; 17 to 1 between 1778 and 1878

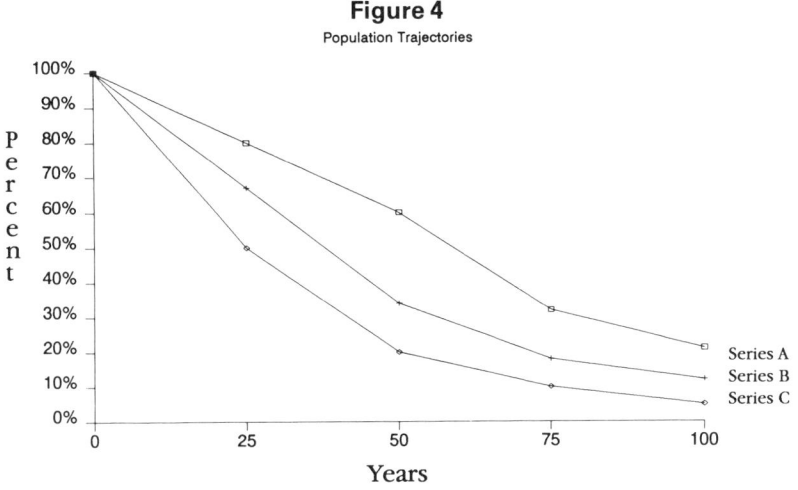

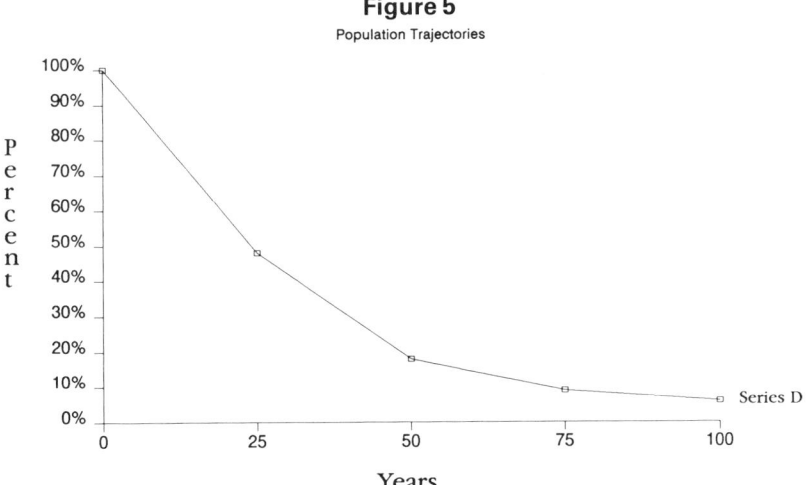

Notes:
Series A = Schmitt's trajectory for Hawai'i based on 1778 population of 225,000
Series B = Trajectory for Hawai'i based on King's estimate of a 1778 population of 400,000
Series C = Low average trajectory for all indigenous populations surveyed
Series D = Trajectory of native Hawaiian population (including part-Hawaiian) based on a 1778 population of 800,000

would be more in keeping with the experiences of a host of other comparable first-contact situations, while 20 to 1 or more would seem most likely if the calculation is based on the native population in the 1890s instead of 1878. Of course, if Hawai'i, with its high percentage of coastal population suffered in those locales anything even remotely like other coastal populations that have been studied, the projected pre-*haole* population would soar considerably higher.

Some final points on this section. I noted earlier that, contrary to the contention of Schmitt and many previous writers, it is now recognized that contemporary estimates of indigenous populations during the early years of European contact—estimates by natives and non-natives alike—were, if anything, generally conservative. In view of this, it is instructive to look at three documents from the 19th century. Although, individually, none of them is more than suggestive, taken together—and added to everything else we have reviewed—they all point in a single direction and add some anecdotal support to the matters at hand. The first document was published in 1848. Two years earlier Hawai'i's Minister of Foreign Relations, R. C. Wyllie, had circulated a lengthy questionnaire to the islands' missionaries. Among the questionnaire's more than one hundred specific queries, one sought to determine the potential population that each district in the islands might sustain "if properly cultivated" and another sought estimates of "the greatest population that ever existed in the district."

In some respects, of course, the missionaries were not the best people to ask this sort of question. They were living in their assigned districts at a time when, some of them reported, the annual number of deaths routinely was at least double the number of births—an astonishing demographic phenomenon. In many years (including those during which these estimates were being made) the death/birth ratio was much worse even than that. Moreover, those few children who survived the early years of life surrounded by "parents and nurses [who] are almost all diseased" became "tainted in the blood," observed one writer, "and grow up sickly" to become adults who "lie down and die the easiest of any people with which I am acquainted." Surrounded by "large tracts of land, which were once inhabited and cultivated [and] now lie waste," many missionaries already believed it was "too late to save the nation from extinction."[51] Such a perspective—combined with their often expressed ideological commitment to an image of the Hawaiians as naturally lazy, licentious, unthinking, and uncivilized—hardly encouraged the missionaries to think expansively in terms of potential or past native achievements.

Nevertheless, the missionaries were—literally—closer to that world of the past than any historical records can bring us. And they all reported that, from everything they could learn, the population "of olden time," as one of them put it, was vastly higher than in the 1840s; perhaps four times the present figure, wrote the Reverend J. S. Green from Makawao, Maui; "to say that it was ten times greater would probably fall short of the truth," wrote the Reverend H. R. Hitchcock from Moloka'i. But most of them would not venture numerical guesses, preferring to say merely that the population in the past was "much larger," "vastly greater," "much more numerous," and that "the country was full of people."[52]

On the matter of potential population they were a bit bolder. Some of their estimates were far too low—and one was clearly far too high. But if we piece together and analyze and extrapolate from the varied and scattered and inconsistently formulated estimates (from 30,000 along the 25 mile-long seacoast at Hanalei on Kaua'i to 50,000 for the districts of Ko'olau and Waialua on O'ahu to "probably five times its present population, or more" for Wailuku on Maui to Reverend Hitchcock's guess of at least ten times the current population on Moloka'i—and so on) the numbers climb into the vicinity of 750,000 to 800,000, without counting large chunks of the islands from which no reports were received and for which extrapolation from other district reports is too hazardous.[53]

The second 19th century document that deserves some attention is the journal of missionary William Ellis when he visited the island of Hawai'i in the summer of 1823. Ellis reported the island's population at about 85,000 (as others had) and noted that, according to the natives—some of whom had lived through the entire post-Cook era and most of whom at least had parents born in pre-*haole* times—the population of that island was then only one-quarter of what it had been forty-five years earlier—almost precisely what the best modern scholarship would retrospectively predict.[54] [See Figure 4, series "C".] If both of those assessments were even close to the truth, and if the all-island population distribution was not vastly different then and in 1778 as it was at the time of the first relatively careful census in 1831–32, the per-island and total island population of Hawai'i in 1778 and 1823 would have been roughly as follows:

Island	1778	1823
Hawai'i	340,000	85,000
Maui	260,331	65,082
O'ahu	220,927	55,231
Kaua'i	81,502	20,375
Moloka'i	44,549	11,137
Lāna'i	11,879	2,970
Ni'ihau	7,774	1,944
Kaho'olawe	594	149
Total	967,556	241,888

Compared with the most frequently-cited estimate for 1823, James Jackson Jarves's "loose estimate" (made in 1843) of 142,050 for all the islands—itself based on the hearsay report of missionary C. S. Stewart—the most problematically high of the above figures for 1823 are those for Maui, O'ahu, Kaua'i, and Moloka'i. But—and this is crucial—the Jarves/Stewart numerical guesses for those islands' 1823 populations are as much as 43 percent *lower* than the actual census count of 1831–32, whereas the overall trajectory of change shows that in every case their populations *must* have been substantially *higher* in 1823 than in 1832. (The island of Hawai'i's population, according to those figures, declined substantially between 1823 and 1832, consistent with the overall change trajectory.)[55] In short, Stewart's hearsay, which became Jarves's "loose estimate" for the 1823 all-island population, *had* to have been a gross underestimate. And the proof is in the unvarying overall trajectory of the missionaries' own censal records.

Just how much of an underestimate the Jarves/Stewart figures for 1823 represent is impossible to say with any precision. And, of course, the results might have differed from island to island: O'ahu, for example, suffered a disproportionately high rate of decline prior to 1823 due in large part to what was probably the worst epidemic ever recorded in Hawai'i—the catastrophic *ma'i 'ōku'u* or "squatting sickness"—variously thought to have been cholera, typhoid fever, or bubonic plague.[56] Thus, O'ahu's population may well have declined by more than 75 percent by 1823 and thus the island may have had fewer people at that time than is suggested by the above figures. On the other hand, migration to O'ahu had begun by this time, offsetting some of the disproportionate loss to disease.

In any case, overall it would seem more than safe to assume that the annual rate of decline between 1823 and 1832 (nine years punctuated by at least three major epidemics) was at *least* as great as the annual rate of decline between the censuses of 1831–32 and 1835–36 (four years with no epidemics). If, then, we use the 1831–32 to 1835–36 rate of decline (when the first two genuine censuses reported a population drop from approximately 130,000 to just over 108,000) to project back a minimum all-island population for 1823 we achieve a total of about 188,000 people in 1823. Any compensation for the epidemics of 1824 to 1826—when, in the words of the native chronicler Samuel M. Kamakau, "thousands died, especially in the country districts" ("the greatest proportion," predictably warned at least one missionary, being "those who neglect instruction")—would raise that number to the general vicinity of 200,000. This is the same rough estimate that Golovnin heard and reported for 1818, as we saw earlier, and it coincides approximately with an 1822 estimate listing the all-island population at "above 200,000."[57] Using the same 4 to 1 depopulation ratio between 1778 and 1823 that is the rate reported to Ellis by the Hawaiians and that is the low average for other similar populations during that stretch of time following European contact, we find a probable 1778 population of about 800,000.

As for the likely 1778 per-island population, the straight-line projection that results in an all-island total of 967,556 (see above) probably overestimates the 1778 populations of Maui and O'ahu, since it provides them each with more than 350 people per square mile—and it certainly underestimates the populations of Hawai'i and Lāna'i, since it provides each of them with only 84 or 85 people per square mile. An adjustment of those estimates, while admittedly only guesswork—like every previous estimate—though taking into consideration the likely differences in island carrying capacities, might result in something like the following:

Island	Estimated 1778 population	Population per square mile
Hawai'i	403,800	100
Maui	123,896	170
O'ahu	121,540	200
Kaua'i	82,995	150
Moloka'i	44,387	170
Lāna'i	13,950	100
Ni'ihau	3,650	50
Kaho'olawe	1,125	25
Total	795,343	123 (average)

One problem with this pattern of settlement (apart from its false appearance of precision which results from the straightforward multiplication of land area by rounded-off guesses as to population per square mile) is that it produces an unexplained differential in the post-*haole* rate of population decline, with O'ahu and Maui faring relatively much better than the other islands between 1778 and the first missionary census of 1831–32—while, as just noted, O'ahu in fact suffered an especially high rate of decline due to the infamous *ma'i 'ōku'u* epidemic. This differential could be because the 1778 populations of O'ahu and Maui were in fact higher than the numbers posited here and/or—as also mentioned above—because of the large migrations to Honolulu and Lahaina from the other islands that began even before the 1820s when those port towns became commercial centers. This migration was frequently commented on by Western visitors and residents—and frequently lamented by such missionaries as Isaac Bliss as late as 1844 when, in his mission station report from the island of Hawai'i, he deplored the "irresistable, & to multitudes, the fatal tide of emigration to O'ahu" and "the pestilential atmosphere of the metropolis."[58] What all this indicates is that, although all the evidence plainly points to a 1778 archipelagic population in the vicinity of 800,000 or more, much additional work will have to be done on the question of individual island populations.*

Finally, the third suggestive document from this era is an 1839 article written by the Hawaiian historian David Malo, entitled "On the Decrease of Population in the Hawaiian Islands." In that article, Malo—who was born in 1793—wrote: "In the reign of Kamehameha, from the time I was born until I was nine years old, the pestilence visited the Hawaiian Islands, and the majority of the people from Hawai'i to Ni'ihau [that is, all the inhabited islands] died." Malo turned nine years of age in 1802—two years before the great epidemic that swept O'ahu and elsewhere. If Malo's assertion was even close to being correct (as many 19th century Hawaiians and non-Hawaiians believed even before Malo's article appeared),[59] it adds the following coincidental dimension to our overall considerations.

Thus far, from a variety of angles—from internal critiques of King's early estimate and modern calculations of conventional depopulation ratios to extrapolations from the testimony of 19th century Hawaiians and missionaries—we have found a population of about 800,000 occurring again and again at the low to moderate end of our 1778 population projections. If we take that figure and apply Malo's contention of at least a 50 percent loss by 1802 (assuming again the most conservative reading of his statement— that is, that "majority" means no more than "half" and that the depopulation he described covered the 24 years since 1778 and not just the nine years following his birth), we arrive at a population of about 400,000 a quarter of a century after Western contact, but before the great epidemic of 1804–1805. (Drastic as this decline

---

*As this monograph goes to press I have just begun a review of the likely population in an area of nine *ahupua'a* (sub-districts) covering one half of a single traditional district *(moku* or *kalana)* on O'ahu. (The island had 86 *ahupua'a* within six major districts.) My preliminary estimate, based on apparent levels of pre-1778 taro production, is that the *half* district in question produced enough taro to support a population at least 3 to 5 times as large as the number conventionally estimated for the entire district and within the range Schmitt estimates as the total population of O'ahu. In fact, just *three* of these *ahupua'a*—Waiāhole, He'eia, and Kailua—produced enough taro to feed over 20,000 people, while Schmitt estimates the population of all the island's 86 *ahupua'a* at between 35,000 and 50,000. The inescapable conclusion is that the conventional estimate for this district's pre-*haole* population size—like the conventional estimates of O'ahu's and the entire archipelago's pre-*haole* population—is woefully understated.

magnitude is, it is less than would be achieved merely by applying the average annual rate of decline measured in the epidemic-free early 1830s to the 1778–1804 period—so it is hardly an unlikely possibility.) If we chart this decline along with the probable population of about 200,000 in 1823 and the subsequent census counts from 1832, 1836, 1850, 1853, 1860, 1866, 1872, and 1878—a century after contact—the graph follows almost precisely the downward trend common in other comparable settings. [Compare Figure 5 with series "C" in Figure 4.]

III

Some Likely Objections

If the population of Hawai'i in 1778 was less than 800,000 the burden of proof now clearly resides with those who would hold to that opinion. Every indicator—from close examination of the flaws in King's estimate to the potential and likelihood of pre-*haole* growth rates, from the minimum carrying capacity of the islands to minimal expected depopulation ratios following Western contact—establishes 800,000 as a low to moderate estimate. Compared with the data and analysis underlying this estimate, support for the traditional estimates of 200,000 to 300,000 rests on just that—tradition—and nothing more. It seems likely, in fact, that a figure higher than 800,000, rather than one lower than this, will result from detailed future research.

This assertion is at such variance with the conventional wisdom on the subject that there will no doubt arise an instinctive reaction against it—a reaction that should, however, subside once the data are scrutinized. Nevertheless, three possible objections are sufficiently likely to be raised that they deserve mention here. One of them would challenge the likelihood of a growth rate producing the numbers I consider to be minimal; another would resurrect the notion that the Hawaiian population peaked a century prior to European contact (presumably because of limited resources) and was already in sharp decline when Cook arrived; the third would object to the probability of a depopulation rate as severe as the one I have postulated.

The first objection follows the common belief that, whatever the natural growth of Hawai'i's pre-*haole* population, it was kept in check, as demographer Eleanor C. Nordyke has summarized it, by "warfare, infanticide, abortion, sacrificial killing, and limited health measures."[1] Of these, only infanticide and abortion—if practiced with extraordinary frequency—could have an effect sufficient to reduce dramatically the population projection suggested in these pages. But first, what about those other supposed population growth restraints?

As for "limited health measures," almost twenty years ago microbiologist O. A. Bushnell showed in some detail that the kapu system in ancient Hawai'i was "remarkably effective" in maintaining a high level of hygiene and sanitation, with the result that "the aboriginal Hawaiians were an extraordinarily healthy people, who were afflicted with no important infectious diseases in the centuries of isolation which intervened between the end of their intercourse with Tahiti and the time of their discovery by Captain Cook." Two hundred years earlier James King and others made similar observations. The Hawaiians, wrote King, "are exceedingly cleanly at their meals and their mode of dressing both their animal and vegetable food, was universally allowed to be greatly superior to ours." Added Archibald Campbell, one of the first Westerners to live in Hawai'i: "The natives . . . are extremely cleanly in their persons. . . . The houses . . . are kept very clean, and their household utensils, consisting of wooden dishes and calabashes, are hung, neatly arranged, upon the walls. . . . In all of [the houses] the utmost attention to cleanliness prevails."[2]

The foods and health habits of the Hawaiians were far more salubrious than those of their European contempories and were even superior to those of modern Americans in their diets' nutritional value and relative lack of saturated fat, cholesterol, sugar, and sodium—and, of course, in the absence from their lives of alcohol and tobacco. Not suprisingly, examinations of ancient skeletal remains have reported routinely that the Hawaiians were an exceptionally well nourished, strong, and vigorous people. In addition, paleopathological studies of pre-1778 Hawaiian skeletons reveal what one eminent pathologist has called the "astonishing" ability of the Hawaiians to set bone fractures without infection and with a competence that would be "excellent even today," adding that "in almost every instance [of nearly 900 skeletons studied] the fracture is so well healed that it could not have been the cause of death."[3] Moreover, as discussed earlier (Chapter 2, note 20), it is now almost certain that Hawaiians in 1778 had life expectancies greater than their European contemporaries (who were themselves at the time in the take-off phase of a major population explosion) and also greater than the conventional paleodemographic estimates of their own life expectancies that have been conducted to date. And finally, it should be recalled that the great strides in public health that have been accomplished during the past century throughout much of the world were based largely upon the conquest of infectious diseases which the Hawaiians had never had, but that had devastated Europe for centuries. "Limited health measures" became a serious problem in Hawai'i, affecting population growth, only after the coming of the West and the subsequent importation of infectious disease, the disruption of nutritional patterns, and the collapse of the hygiene-maintaining *kapu* system.

The matter of sacrificial killing is similarly ineffective in reducing our posited growth rate. There is no good evidence to indicate the amount of pre-*haole* human sacrifice that occurred, but it clearly was never practiced on a scale resembling that of ancient Mexico or other areas of supposedly wholesale killing. (One very reliable and very early Western visitor to Hawai'i mentioned that he had heard of the practice of human sacrifice, but admitted that "nothing of the kind took place during my stay"—and his stay lasted 13 months. There is, in fact, in the early traveler descriptions of Hawai'i, a remarkable absence of first-hand accounts of this supposedly common practice.) In addition, it is known that pigs and other animals were frequently substituted for humans in the ceremonies, that usually "law breakers or war victims" who had already been executed or killed in battle were selected when a human victim was to be chosen for consecration ("sacrifice," in its colloquial sense, is in fact a misnomer here), and that the practice itself was of relatively late historical origin. Beyond these matters, however, is the singularly crucial fact that women were not sacrificed or consecrated because menstruation made them symbolically defiled beings.[4] This last point minimizes to virtual non-existence the impact of sacrifice on population growth, since Hawai'i was not a monogamous culture and it is women, after all, who bear the children of the next generation.

The same holds true for warfare. Although there is little doubt that ancient Hawaiian chiefs engaged in fairly frequent wars in their quest for greater status and *mana*, there is no good evidence of a high death rate from such pre-*haole* (and low technology) warfare. Indeed, paleopathological analyses of skeletal damage occasioned by trauma points to an extremely *low* level of death from violence attributable to war, something that is very common among indigenous peoples for whom warfare often is more a ritual quest for status than a bloodthirsty means of conquest. Moreover, if the supposedly devastating wars of the late 18th century post-*haole* era are taken to represent what was at the time considered a high level of death from warfare, it is clear from our earlier discussion of that era (see the latter part of note 50 in Chapter 2) that "normal" warfare would not seriously have affected the population growth rate. In addition to the fact that our presumed growth rate was set at a bare minimum (0.52 percent per annum) to accomodate catastrophes of one sort or another, warfare does not historically have the negative effect on population growth that popular thought supposes, in large part because the high ratio of male over female deaths in most wartime struggles allows for rapid population replacement.

Take the case of Britain during the decade of 1911–1921, which includes the years of the most destructive war in British history and the devastating influenza pandemic of 1918–1919: in 1911 the population was approximately 40.8 million; by 1921 it had *increased* to 42.7 million—despite the loss of an estimated 2.4 million people due to the war, outmigration, influenza, other excess civilian deaths, and projected loss of births. Many equally dramatic examples abound. To cite just two prominent more recent examples: between 1940 and 1950, the population of Japan increased by almost 14 percent—an annual rate of increase, during the midst of the Second World War, that is almost triple the rate I am proposing for Hawai'i during most of the pre-*haole* era; in Southeast Asia between 1960 and 1970, a decade of war so intense that it has often been described as genocidal, the population increased more than five times as fast as my proposed pre-*haole* Hawai'i growth rate.[5] In sum, there is simply no support for the notion that pre-1778 warfare acted as a population growth check in Hawai'i, particularly in view of the fact that there is no evidence at all of a high mortality rate from whatever wars did occur.

That leaves infanticide and abortion. While it is known that Hawaiians used various techniques both to induce abortion and to increase fertility, we have no good evidence one way or another to indicate the extent of these practices. And we probably never will. But infanticide has long been believed to have been rampant in ancient Hawai'i. The myth of the slaughter of innocents—which I have explored at length in a separate essay—began with the missionaries, such as the Rev. Samuel Bartlett ("Two thirds of all the children, probably, were destroyed in infancy—strangled or buried alive") and has been repeated uncritically, and almost always with no effort to produce supporting citations, by respectable scholars such as anthropologist Patrick V. Kirch up to the present ("There is some evidence [none is given] that by European contact the Hawaiians were actively practicing several methods of population control, including abortion and infanticide").[6] But in fact there is not a *single* piece of credible evidence that infanticide existed on a significant scale as a cultural practice in pre-*haole* Hawai'i—and there *is* positive evidence that it did not exist as such. Consider the following.

In his journal entry for February 4, 1779—while Cook's ships were leaving the island of Hawai'i, temporarily, as it turned out, to Cook's bad luck—the *Discovery*'s surgeon, David Samwell, took time to reflect on all he had seen, from the stature and dress of the Hawaiians to their ritual prohibitions and methods of fishing and cultivation, from their medical practices to their general dispositions. It was a careful effort of the sort Samwell is known for, and in it he was perfectly clear about one thing in particular: the people of Hawai'i were "totally unacquainted with" the "horrid Custom" of infanticide that was common in other parts of the world—particularly common, though Samwell did not mention it, in England and France. Moreover, he added, "such a great number of fine lively Children that used to play about us every time we went on shore we never saw at any other place during this Voyage." Similar observations were made by others.[7]

More than twenty years later—though almost twenty years, as well, before the arrival of the first missionaries and their preconceived notions of Hawaiian savagery—visitor John Turnbull noted again "the absence from Owhyhee of the horrid practice of infant murder," and added in another context a fact that independently supported the observation: "the women, according to Mr. Young's account, are said to be more numerous than the men," a point that finds confirmation in the skeletal remains of pre-*haole* burials. Along with this, consider Lieutenant King's observation in 1779 that there were "more deformed people [in Hawai'i] than in all the other [Pacific] Islands put together"—an observation echoed by subsequent pre-missionary visitors as late as 1818—and remember that it is, of course, females and the congenitally malformed who are conventionally the first victims of infanticide.[8]

According to Mary Kawena Pukui, commonly regarded as the best modern Hawaiian source for orally-transmitted ancient Hawaiian tradition, "infanticide was occasionally practiced as an easy way out of a difficult personal impasse," on the same sort of furtive and individual level that it is in most societies—including the West in the late 20th century—but the only sanctioned occasion was to prevent "adulteration of the purity of *ali'i* [chiefly] blood lines," when a mixed-class pregnancy occurred. However, this hardly occurred with sufficient frequency to be termed "population control" or to affect the entire society's rate of population growth.[9]

Finally, contrary to unsupported and offhand remarks such as Patrick Kirch's comment that the Hawaiians had "a fairly high rate of infant mortality," the skeletal remains from pre-*haole* Hawai'i that have been studied show an extraordinarily *low* occurrence of infants among them. Of 1171 skeletons studied at the Mōkapu burial site on O'ahu, and 332 skeletons examined at Keōpū on the island of Hawai'i—the only large sites from which detailed information is available—only 4.35 percent at Mōkapu and 3.9 percent at Keōpū were beyond the fetal stage and less than one year old. This produces an infant mortality rate, from all causes, natural and unnatural, about one-ninth of what was common in mid-18th century England and barely a third of what would be found from a survey of American cemeteries in the early 20th century! To be sure, it is possible that some pre-*haole* infant skeletons did not survive and/or that some were not buried as others were at these sites. On the other hand, the death rate for individuals under the age of 15 is also remarkably low at both widely separated sites, thus supporting the overall observation of the healthfulness of Hawaiian children and young adults—and skeletal series from much older sites in other countries have been used to confirm high infant mortality rates. As the most recent paleopathological study of ancient Hawaiian remains observes, the traditional stories "of widespread infanticide . . . are hard to reconcile with documentary and physical evidence" to the contrary.[10] What the ancient Hawaiian remains seem to be trying to tell us, against all our ethnocentric skepticism, is what living Hawaiians have said repeatedly for over a century and a half: in pre-*haole* times the Hawaiians were an extraordinarily healthy people. An undercount of infant remains, for whatever reason, is still a possibility, given the extremely low infant mortality apparent in these burials, but the fact is that *no* evidence exists of either culturally sanctioned large-scale infanticide or a high infant mortality rate in pre-*haole* times —and all the existing evidence in fact points in precisely the opposite direction.

In this same area of challenging the posited pre-*haole* population growth rate, a recent article on Maori demographic change raises questions that conceivably could be imported to the Hawaiian situation. Arguing that dietary inadequacy and other factors may have caused a low fertility rate among pre-*pakeha* (pre-*haole*) Maori women—an entire hypothesis trembling on the edge of a dubious hunch or two regarding the age at onset of menstruation for pre-*pakeha* Maori women and some very questionable osteological assumptions regarding life expectancy and average number of births per woman—Douglas G. Sutton attempts to explain why he believes "there were *only* [his emphasis] 125–175,000 people in New Zealand at the time of European arrival." Whether Sutton's efforts stand up to scrutiny in their New Zealand context I shall leave to others to discuss in detail. (But see my comments, in note 11 below, on the frailty of his method for ascertaining the crucial data on fertility.) In Hawai'i, however, none of Sutton's major demonstrable assumptions, from late age at menarche to low nutritional levels, is supportable. Even if they were, however, as Fekri A. Hassan has shown in a detailed computer simulation, a poorly nourished population with an extremely late average age at menarche of 18 years (plus an additional two years of "adolescent sterility"), an average life expectancy rate for adult females of 31 years, and a 28 month birth interval will produce more than 5.14 children per female, including an average of more than 2.5 daughters. The population growth impact of this scenario is, of course, mitigated by infant and childhood mortality; however, even a more than 50 percent preadult mortality rate—substantially worse than in the tragic environments of Bangladesh or Kampuchea today—would produce a population growth rate *higher* than the minimal rate of 0.52 percent per annum that I have proposed.[11] And, to repeat, this is to impose growth restraints that flatly did not exist in pre-*haole* Hawai'i.

The second general objection that might be raised to the figures proposed earlier has, like the myth of unrestrained infanticide, a long history throughout the Pacific; this is the idea that the population was already declining precipitously long before Western contact. From one end of the Pacific to the other—from New Zealand's Reverend J. F. H. Wohlers's declaration that the Maori, in their "groveling animalism," had long ago "outlived their time" to Hawai'i's equally Reverend Rufus Anderson comparing the deaths of the Hawaiians to "the amputation of diseased members of the body"—colonizing Westerners in the 19th century found the notion of the "natural" decline of the native population a convenient salve to the collective conscience, as they observed the horrific results on the native peoples of the diseases the Westerners had brought with them. It is almost fifty years since Andrew Lind properly disposed of this myth in Hawai'i, but a new variation seems on the verge of creeping into some popular misreadings of recent archaeological research.[12] It needs to be dealt with before it takes hold once again.

The research in question was conducted initially by archaeologist Robert J. Hommon and has been followed up by others. It has found residential-site evidence possibly suggestive of population decline in certain locations in Hawai'i, beginning in the 17th century. In reviewing these studies Patrick Kirch recently has concluded that "it is not certain" and "it cannot be ascertained on the available data" whether the apparent decline in material evidence for population is attributable to actual population decline or merely to population movement from one area to another. (It should be noted that in an earlier piece Kirch was so convinced that the population was declining prior to Western contact that he accompanied his argument with a graph that dramatically charted a "hypothetical" rate of decline so steep that, if unchecked, it would have resulted in the extinction of the Hawaiian people by the mid-19th century, even without Western contact.)[13] In fact, while there rarely ever is "certainty" on subjects such as this, there is no reason whatsoever to hold to a pre-*haole* population decline hypothesis.

Kirch himself points out (as did Hommon) that the sites in question are all in arid and agriculturally marginal areas, while similar research in other areas—and for the archipelago as a whole—show the population increasing at a rapid pace until Cook's arrival in 1778; indeed, that research shows a growth rate substantially *higher* than the one I have proposed here. In addition to the archaeological data on this matter, historical-anthropological information reinforces the point. The Hommon/Kirch hypothesis, after all, is dependent upon a single crucial factor—resource depletion. If the population was declining prior to Western contact it had to have been because, as Kirch puts it, "the capacity of the indigenous technological productive system to support increased population had reached its limits." Indeed, for the population to begin the serious decline that Kirch proposes, that productive system must have done much more than "reach its limits." The examples noted earlier of wartime Britain, Japan, and Southeast Asia, as well as those of Ireland during the century ending with the potato blight and plague-ravaged 15th and 16th century England, clearly show how cataclysmic events must be for an otherwise expanding population actually to decline: as we saw, all of those populations grew steadily during the worst of times.

For a hypothesis of population decline as a result of resource depletion in 17th and 18th century Hawai'i thus to make any sense at all, it is essential that its proponents produce evidence of severe malnutrition and other consequences of drastic food shortage in the late pre-*haole* era. There is, of course, no such evidence. On the contrary, in addition to the paleopathological studies, which are unanimous in their portrayal of an extraordinarily strong and well-nourished people at the level of both chief and commoner, there is the historical evidence of the earliest Western explorers who found in Hawai'i an extremely robust people with a high ratio of children to adults (a low child/adult ratio is typical in societies suffering from resource depletion sufficient to reduce population levels), and a people who were drawing sustenance from what seemed to be a literal cornucopia. Cook's men constantly commented on what seemed an inexhaustible supply of foodstuffs, as when George Gilbert observed that "everything was as plentifull the last Day, as when we first came in." Or, as Captain Clerke put it, after noting that "both pork & roots [taro, yams, and sweet potatoes] are to be got almost anywhere among this cluster of Isles": "We never saw, nor from what we did see, could we form any idea that any Isles whatever could have so much provision to spare and still themselves abound, which is the case here." The fact that the population was so huge that many people, on all the islands, were forced to live in agriculturally marginal areas, says nothing about these people's ability to survive in such areas; there is, simply, no evidence that they did not thrive despite difficult environmental surroundings.[14]

Moreover, populations faced with declining resources sufficient to require population control typically develop cultural patterns that were markedly absent in Hawai'i—patterns including culturally sanctioned high rates of infanticide and tight restrictions on sexual behavior, especially frequency of intercourse. We have already seen that there is no evidence of a high rate of pre-*haole* infanticide. In addition, if there is one thing on which no one has ever disagreed regarding Hawai'i at the time of Western contact, it is that it was a place of free and open sexuality—an "Aphrodisian" society, as Marshall Sahlins has put it. And finally, it has recently been demonstrated that societies faced with conditions of scarcity tend to restrict their rate of strenuous leisure activities, thus reducing unnecessary caloric expenditures.[15] Once again, as is well known, the opposite situation prevailed in Hawai'i. Nothing was more vividly described by the awe-struck Western visitors than the boxing matches, surfing contests, dance extravaganzas, and other vigorous (and calorie-consuming) leisure-time pursuits of the Hawaiians. And these were activities, it must be recalled, that were full-time daily routines during the annual Makahiki Festival which lasted for *four months* of each year; no people facing a situation of severely limited resources is either likely or able to give over a third of each year to such festivities.

In sum, whatever the reason for the minor site habitation phenomenon uncovered by Hommon and others—and the location of the sites in the least habitable areas of the islands plainly suggests simple migration caused by temporary soil exhaustion or seasonal drought—pre-*haole* population decline is an idea that is at least half a century out of date. All the evidence plainly indicates that the pre-*haole* Hawaiian population, large as it was, had not yet approached the upper asymptote of the logistic curve—in layman's terms, the top of the S-curve—that commonly describes natural population growth. That event, however, did arrive—with shocking suddenness—as soon as the Western plagues were loosed among the people.

The third possible objection to the population estimate proposed here, like the first two objections, has its origins in the early years of Hawaiian-European contact. After first coming upon the Hawaiian islands, Cook's ships spent just two weeks in late January and early February of 1778 at Kaua'i and Ni'ihau, whereupon they left to explore the northwest coast of North America. Returning to Hawai'i ten months later, they found an epidemic of venereal disease spreading among the people of Maui and the island of Hawai'i—the opposite end of the archipelago from Kaua'i. Wrote William Ellis: "We found the venereal disease raging among these poor people, in a violent degree, some of whom were infected most terribly; and it was the opinion of most, that we, in our former visit, had been the cause of this irreparable injury." James King agreed with Ellis on the source of the epidemic, though he noted that "this is a disputed point amongst us, considering the Distance between Atoui [Kaua'i] & here, & the short time since we were there." Perhaps, some thought, the disease had been present before their arrival. This was, of course, just a local variation on a debate that had gripped Europe two centuries earlier: where had this horrible disease come from?[16]

In Hawai'i, however, it was a short-lived debate. Whereas both 15th and 16th century Europe and the "New World" that had just then been encountered suffered from what at the time appeared to be a new disease on both continents, by the latter 18th century syphilis and gonorrhea were so widespread in the West that the single most common advertisements in 18th century London periodicals were for spurious "cures" for venereal disease. In fact, not counting the numerous men in whom syphilis was at that moment in an early latent stage—that is, contagious, but not evident, a stage that can last for several years—Cook's crews were so enfeebled by venereal disease just before leaving Tahiti for Hawai'i that there were "scarce hands enough able to do duty on board." More than half the crew was too sick from V.D. to work. In short, once the evidence was weighed—including the Hawaiians' insistence that the disease had not been present in their land before the coming of Cook—there could be no doubt as to the source of the infection. (This early recognition that venereal disease was absent in pre-*haole* Hawai'i has since been confirmed by the paleopathological study of ancient Hawaiian remains.) Moreover, it is now clear that the Hawaiians moved among their islands with amazing speed and ease: for example, although the *Resolution* and *Discovery* left the island of Hawai'i barely a week after Cook's death, news of the event long preceded them as they wound their way toward Kaua'i before heading toward open sea; indeed, teenage Hawaiian girls aboard the two ships at that time were sufficiently knowledgeable of the other islands to direct the Europeans to harbors with which they were familiar.[17] This same ease of travel, of course, also helped spread disease with great speed.

But venereal disease was not all that Cook's ships brought; they also brought tuberculosis, an influenza virus or some other deadly upper respiratory infection, and no doubt a good deal more. The men aboard those ships were, as Captain Clerke described them, "infernal and dissolute," largely recruited from the dregs of English society. Though they may have been (or at least superficially appeared to be) momentarily free of the infections that were rife in England when they signed on to sail to the Pacific, these men were the biological hosts as well as the cultural representatives of a society that was at that exact moment in the midst of a smallpox epidemic and in which more than three out of four deaths were being caused by typhus, typhoid fever, measles, smallpox, bronchitis, whooping cough, tuberculosis, and "convulsions." Indeed, Cook had left England at a time when, in addition to the smallpox epidemic, tuberculosis morbidity was reaching a peak never equalled before or since.[18]

By the turn of the 19th century, note René and Jean Dubos, "half of the English population had [tuberculosis]," and the mortality rate in 1778 was rapidly ascending to the point where, in barely two decades, nearly a third of all deaths in London would be caused by T.B. It was appropriately called "The Great White Plague"—and for the Hawaiians and other Pacific islanders that phrase had more than one meaning. In fact, so diseased was Cook's crew during their stay in Hawai'i that at one point they took part of a *heiau*, a sacred Hawaiian place of worship, and converted it to "an hospital for our sick." Subsequent ship captains also sent their sick ashore, where, as Captain Portlock was to note, they were "treated exceedingly well by the natives." The full list of specific diseases that those men were carrying will never be known for certain. But, in addition to the ship's crews spreading V.D. and upper respiratory infections, we do know that (among others) Captain Clerke himself, the commander of the *Discovery* in 1778–1779, was in close contact with Hawaiians from Kaua'i, Hawai'i, Maui, O'ahu, probably Lāna'i, and possibly Moloka'i (either by going ashore or by meeting them on board his ship) all the while that he was struggling with the final stages of a fatal case of tuberculosis. The "exceedingly" helpful natives of those islands did not know, of course, that certain types of tuberculosis can be more contagious even than measles.[19]

None of these diseases—venereal disease, tuberculosis, or influenza—have the same effect on populations that first contract them as they do on populations that have had to live with them for generations. We saw earlier the effect that tuberculosis had on an isolated Canadian Indian tribe: nearly 10 percent mortality per year until more than half the population was dead—and for most of that time the disease was only identifiable as tuberculosis by microscopic examination, so confusing and misleading were the early symptoms before the disease settled into its familiar pattern. A similar reaction in Hawai'i would have cut the population in half before the next group of Europeans arrived in 1786. And there is now some admittedly preliminary reason to believe that—in addition to a lack of acquired immunity—the Hawaiians and other Polynesians may have had bronchial cilia lacking certain structures that might have helped in the resistance against respiratory diseases, including tuberculosis in relation to bronchiectasis. If so, it is likely that the cilia simply did not evolve in Polynesians as they did in Europeans because in their benign Pacific environment such genetic defense was unnecessary. It is common for genetic traits that are functional and beneficial in one environment to become dangerously dysfunctional in a new environment, probably the most well-known example being the so-called "thrifty genotype hypothesis" connecting post-European contact diabetes susceptibility among some indigenous peoples with a favorable genetically evolved ability to withstand greatly varying availabilities of food supplies. In any case, throughout the 19th century European physicians observed that tuberculosis, including tuberculosis of the joints and glands, had an astonishingly deadly effect on children brought from the Pacific for European educations: such children "almost uniformly" contracted tuberculosis, wrote the prestigious British medical journal *The Lancet* in 1824: "they bear the first winter tolerably well, but droop during the second, and the third generally proves fatal to them." The same observation was made in a major 1883 treatise on tuberculosis, and well into the second half of the 20th century Hawaiians and other Polynesians had much higher rates of tuberculosis than did other ethnic groups that had immigrated to the Pacific.[20]

A similar pattern follows the history of syphilis. When it first appeared in Europe, the disease that later would be characterized by a slow debilitation of its host, "struck like a thunderbolt," writes medical historian Alfred Crosby, sweeping from London to Moscow in five years. It rapidly attacked and destroyed its victims' "body, palate, uvula, jaw, and tonsils. . . . Large gummy tumors were common, and the victim suffered agonizing pains in muscles and nerves, especially at night. General physical deterioration followed and often culminated in early death." Within thirty years or so following its first appearance, however, the malignancy of the disease began to abate; it settled in and gradually evolved into a slow, long-term killer—frequently marked by latency and remission.[21] But in Hawai'i, even more so than in Europe, it wreaked havoc on the population for more than a century.

At the same time that syphilis, tuberculosis, and other diseases were slaughtering the already living generations of Hawaiians, syphilis and gonorrhea were destroying fetuses and the fertility of the population, and thus its ability to recover. The devastating effect of gonorrhea on fertility is well known; what is less well known is that, even today, there is virtually "no chance that an infant will be born normal and healthy" if its mother has primary or secondary syphilis during her pregnancy and that about one out of three fetuses infected with syphilis will either miscarry or be stillborn. Even less well known is the fact that tuberculosis can greatly reduce fertility and that genital tuberculosis—which has been estimated as present in as many as one-third of tuberculosis victims in developing countries—"almost always causes primary sterility in affected men and women."[22]

In 1778 and 1779, those sailing with Cook found in Hawai'i a people "above the middle size, strong and well made & of a dark copper Colour . . . upon the whole a fine handsome sett of People"—a people vastly populous and whose "abundant stock of Children promised very fairly a plentiful supply for the next Generation." As we have seen, these first hand observations are confirmed by the modern study of pre-*haole* era skeletons which indicate an extraordinarily healthy people whose children survived at an exceptionally high rate and whose adult bodies—male and female alike—were "slender . . . in spite of heavy musculature," whose men characteristically had "massive" arm, back, and leg muscles, and whose women possessed a "sturdiness and muscular development quite beyond that of the usual European representation of the female body."[23]

In 1786, seven years after Cook's ships had left the islands, the next European ship—the French frigate *La Boussole*—reached Hawai'i. The surgeon aboard that ship found the residents of Maui, where Cook had not even landed, covered with:

> buboes, and scars which result from their supperating, warts, spreading ulcers with caries of the bones, nodes, exostoses, fistula, tumors of the lachrymal and salival ducts, scrofulous swellings, inveterate opthalmiae, ichorous ulcerations of the tunica conjuctiva, atrophy of the eyes, blindness, inflamed prurient herpetic eruptions, indolent swellings of the extremities, and among children, scald head, or a malignant tinea, from which exudes a fetid and acrid matter. . . . [T]*he greater part* of these unhappy victims of sensuality, when arrived at the age of nine or ten, were feeble and languid, exhausted by marasmus, and affected with the rickets.[24]

This observation was made on a remote part of the island, "affording neither water nor wood," and that was "little frequented by navigators." Still, scores of people greeted the ship in canoes and on the shore, "most of them [revealing] traces of the ravages occasioned by the venereal disease." These included "children of seven or eight years of age"—too young to have contracted it sexually, but just the right age to have been those of the first generation who had survived birth with congenital syphilis passed on by mothers who had slept with infected members of Cook's crews, or —more likely in this area—with Hawaiian men who had been infected by those women, or by women who had been infected by men who had slept with those women. Even today, after centuries of infection-mitigating exposure to the disease, syphilis will spread from an infected to a non-infected European or American in 20 to 50 percent of heterosexual contacts—a rate 400 to 500 times greater than AIDS.[25] In the pan-sexual society of Hawai'i—with no previous exposure to either syphilis or gonorrhea—the joys of freedom became the route to widespread destruction once the deadly microbes had been introduced.

As for the mention of rickets in the majority of the children, rickets is most commonly caused by a deficiency of vitamin D, insufficient amounts of calcium and phosphorus in the diet, or by certain chronic diseases. (Renal rickets, for example, derives from kidney disease preventing the excretion of phosphates, thus forcing the body to draw mineral from bones with a consequent softening of the skeleton. It is particularly damaging to female children.) Since there is no evidence at all of rickets in the reports from Cook's voyage or in any of the pathological analyses of pre-*haole* era skeletal remains—and since diets would probably not have changed drastically in less than a decade, nor did Hawaiians suffer from an insufficiency of sunlight—this observed epidemic of childhood rickets would seem to have resulted most likely from some virulent intestinal or kidney disease also left behind by Cook's men and/or by skeletal damage resulting from venereal infection.[26]

It is also probable that Cook's ships left influenza behind. In addition to the symptoms recorded by Ellis (note 18 above), some very recent research by British and Soviet scientists on influenza transmission suggests that, as well as through direct contact transmission, influenza is *most* often spread by people who have contracted the disease in the past and then spread it—without coming down with it again themselves—during predictable times of subsequent years, the so-called "flu seasons." It is known that England was in the grip of a major flu epidemic during the entire four to five months leading up to Cook's departure on his final voyage—and that Cook's ships arrived in Hawai'i at precisely the time (in both 1778 and 1779) when contagion among those sailors who had been affected by the English epidemic was likely to be at a peak. If Cook's crews transmitted the virus to the Hawaiians, as they almost surely did, they transmitted what was one of the most lethal killers the Europeans ever bequeathed to indigenous peoples. As Henry Dobyns has pointed out: "In recent decades, influenza has demonstrated that it can almost exterminate tribesmen in the Amazon River basin who have not been exposed to it in its various forms." In one case noted by Dobyns, 300 people in one tribe who were exposed to influenza died of pulmonary edema in 38 hours. Numerous other examples exist of previously isolated peoples losing 15 percent and more of their population—primarily the very young—in a single influenza epidemic. And once introduced, influenza returns to kill again and again and again.[27]

But why this long digression on disease? Because in recent years it has begun to be suggested once again—sometimes directly, sometimes obliquely—that the Hawaiians had some of these infections before the coming of Cook and therefore possessed at least a degree of immunity to them. If these suggestions were correct, they could be raised as objections to the depopulation rate that forms one part of this revised look at Hawai'i's pre-*haole* population level. They are, however, wrong.

The first relatively recent suggestion along these lines was quite direct. In 1978 geographer Peter Pirie proposed that the Hawaiians living in certain parts of the islands—the wet windward coasts—may well have had yaws (a syphilis-related treponemal infection) prior to contact with the Europeans. "If yaws was in fact endemic in the climatically suitable areas of the Hawaiian chain," he claimed, "the young people growing up in a yaws-infested environment would have acquired substantial immunity to venereal infection from syphilis."[28]

First, Pirie's only serious pieces of evidence linking yaws to Hawai'i prior to Western contact are three vague quotations and one relatively detailed account from visitors observing conditions in Hawai'i more than half a century *after* Western contact. There is, in contrast, not a single piece of evidence for yaws or any other treponemal infection among the many accounts of the earliest visitors (until, of course, after they had themselves implanted the diseases), and if there was one thing those sailors knew well it was the symptoms of diseases of this sort. Further, the 19th century descriptions Pirie cites seem, he thinks, to describe yaws rather than syphilis—but at least one of them (the only fairly detailed account) almost certainly is a description of congenital syphilis. That is not exactly a strong case.

Nor is Pirie's suggestion bolstered by studies of the skeletal remains from the major pre-*haole* burial sites at Mōkapu (a wet windward area) or Keōpū. Of more than 1200 individuals studied at these sites specifically in search of evidence for diseases such as yaws and other infections, only one person with a perforated palate and six isolated bones with osteoperiostitis displayed any symptoms that could even marginally be considered possible candidates for yaws. Apart from the fact that other diagnoses are equally plausible in these specimens, the tiny percentage of the population represented by these cases (barely one half of one percent) clearly points in a direction away from infectious yaws or Pirie's "yaws-infested environment." In areas where yaws is endemic, notes Harvard physician and paleopathologist R. T. Steinbock, "as much as 10 to 25 percent of the population will exhibit some form of active yaws." The visible evidence of yaws, which Cook and his crews could not have missed seeing if yaws was then present in Hawai'i, include highly infectious skin lesions all over the body and—particularly in its secondary and tertiary manifestations—gross disfigurement from large, oozing papillomas and bright red facial scars. In addition, more than 80 percent of a population where yaws is present will generally show evidence of past infection. Although this high a percentage of people will not commonly display lesions in their skeletal remains, the percentage that do so is typically at least eight times the total displayed by even the most remotely *suspected* remains at Mōkapu and Keōpū. Thus, even before the discovery and study of 355 skeletons at Keōpū—none of which show any evidence of yaws—the prevailing opinion among paleopathologists was that there is among Hawai'i's pre-*haole* remains "very little evidence suggestive of yaws."²⁹ Today, with the additional evidence from Keōpū, it is clear that there is no credible evidence at all that yaws was present in Hawai'i prior to European contact.

Moreover, even in the almost impossible event that such an infinitesimal percentage of the population did have yaws, its impact on the Hawaiians' immunity to syphilis would have been negligible. As the distinguished British physician for the Royal Navy, Sir James Watt, points out: "If . . . yaws antedated Europeans, syphilitics in the ships would have been protected against yaws, but natives suffering from yaws may not have been immune to syphilis, since cross-immunity develops rapidly in syphilis but takes years to develop in yaws." Indeed, despite the fact that yaws and syphilis are both treponemal infections, the case against yaws providing immunity to syphilis is actually much stronger than Watt implies. The British venereologists, Ambrose King and Claude Nicol, state the matter more plainly: "patients who have suffered from yaws in the past may contract syphilis in later life." As the most recent research on this subject shows, any partial immunity that may occasionally exist is easily overcome by a large inoculum of venereal syphilis—which the generous Hawaiian women were given with a vengeance.³⁰

The other recent suggestion of pre-existing disease among the Hawaiians concerns tuberculosis. It is only the most passing of references, but it needs to be addressed because—despite no supporting evidence at all—it already is becoming part of the conventional popular wisdom. In their examination of the Mōkapu remains some years ago, a pathologist and a physical anthropologist—Lent C. Johnson and Ellis R. Kerley—discovered three vertebrae from one skeleton that displayed symptoms for which tuberculosis was a possible cause, but which also can be produced, they properly noted, by "several organisms." (Although Johnson and Kerley were not specific as to those other possible diagnoses, severe osteoarthritis—which is known to have existed in pre-*haole* Hawai'i—can cause very similar damage to vertebrae.) In any case, there has never been, before or since, a single other indication of anything remotely resembling tuberculosis in pre-*haole* Hawai'i—including the recent study of several hundred skeletons at Keōpū. Given the properly cautious statement of the original diagnosis, combined with the even more important fact that a highly infectious disease like tuberculosis is unlikely to the point of impossibility to occur in what amounts to a miniscule .0006 percent of a sample population (typical populations in which tuberculosis is present will display 75 to 100 times this degree of prevalence in their skeletal remains), it is more than safe to say that tuberculosis was not present in Hawai'i before European contact.[31]

Nevertheless, in his 1974 summary of the Mōkapu study, Charles Snow mentioned "reports" of tuberculosis, citing the 1966 pathological report of William Bowers. But Snow was in error: Bowers's report, in fact, made no such claim. The only mention of the disease in the first-hand paleopathological analyses of pre-*haole* Hawaiian skeletons is in the report by Johnson and Kerley—and they do not make a diagnosis of tuberculosis. Now, however, in his 1985 book, designed as an introductory text on Hawaiian archaeology and prehistory, Patrick Kirch quite blithely includes tuberculosis among "a number of common pathologies" found in pre-*haole* Hawai'i, using Snow's minor and erroneous comment as the basis for his own greatly expanded conclusion. And finally, in his 1987 review of Kirch's book in *The Journal of the Polynesian Society*, Paul L. Cleghorn has escalated this egregious error into the even more grandiose assertion that "prehistoric Hawaiians had generally good health, though *many* suffered from . . . tuberculosis."[32] Let it simply be said here that this statement—having evolved from the smallest speck of the most dubious evidence (from a single skeleton at Mōkapu) to its present position in Kirch's text and Cleghorn's review as a bogus truism—is flatly *un*true, supported as it is by absolutely no good evidence whatsoever. It does, however, make for a good case study of how—even in the world of scholarship—rumor can become transformed into self-substantiating pseudo-fact.

What is the result of all this? First, we have seen that efforts to reduce James King's original estimate of the 1778 Hawaiian population have been founded on little or no solid evidence. In fact, a close review of King's estimate shows that it was far too small. Rather than 400,000, the 1778 population was much more likely to have been 800,000 or more—as evidenced in part by King's lack of knowledge of the windward and inland areas of the islands, as well as by his extrapolation of population density from the island of Hawai'i to the much more thickly-settled older islands. The figure of 800,000, we have again seen, is in fact a modest projection of what could and likely would have been attained by 1778 by a small founding group of settlers landing in the first or second century A.D. if the islands were capable of supporting a population of that size. And we have seen that the islands were capable of such support: there is no doubt that the carrying capacity of the islands—nurtured by the agricultural, aquacultural, and fishing skills of the Hawaiians—was more than sufficient to support a pre-*haole* population of 800,000 or a million or more.

Beyond this, we have learned that the Hawaiians of 1778 were at least as vulnerable as any other previously isolated, extraordinarily healthy indigenous people to the extreme ravages of disease brought by European contact. Indeed, considering the proximity of the vast majority of the population to the coastline, in village settlements, they were probably more vulnerable to depopulation than the native peoples in many other comparable "first contact" situations. Thus, there is no reason to suppose that their rate of depopulation following Western contact was any lower than the norm for such indigenous societies—that is, a decline ratio of at least 20 to 1 from time of contact to nadir, a decline ratio that projects retrospectively from a nadir population of around 40,000 to a 1778 population of roughly between 800,000 and a million. In addition, there is no good evidence whatsoever to support the notion that the Hawaiian population was doing anything other than expanding up to the moment of European contact. Finally, that expansion—which had been occurring for over 1600 years (and possibly much longer), with virtually no outlet for emigration—was unchecked by culturally sanctioned large-scale infanticide or other common population control restrictions, with the possible exception of abortion. And there is no evidence that abortion existed on a scale that would have had any significant impact on population growth; indeed, the high percentage of children in the population encountered by Cook and his men clearly suggests that abortion existed only as a sporadic, individual practice.

The obvious conclusion, then, is that a population for Hawai'i of about 800,000 at the time of Western contact seems a restrained and modest figure. Each individual approach to the question independently leads to this finding; taken together, the combined result of these singular conclusions virtually compels such a judgment.

If, on the other hand, the population of Hawai'i was less than 800,000 in 1778 it is now incumbent on those who would hold this position to demonstrate—*in specific scholarly detail*—precisely how it came to be less than what all the evidence suggests is a minimum.

NOTES

Preface

1. Alfred L. Kroeber, *Cultural and Natural Areas of Native North America,* University of California Publications in American Archaeology and Ethnology, Volume 38 (Berkeley: University of California Press, 1939), Section 11; Angel Rosenblat, *La población indigena y el mestizaje en América* (Buenos Aires: Editorial Nova, 1954). In 1964 Woodrow Borah estimated a figure of "upwards of one hundred million" for the hemisphere in "America as Model: The Demographic Impact of European Expansion Upon the Non-Western World," *Actas y Memorial del XXXV Congreso Internacional de Americanistas* (Mexico City, 1964), III, 381. Then, in 1966, Henry Dobyns published the watershed analysis, "Estimating Aboriginal American Population: An Appraisal of Techniques With a New Hemispheric Estimate," *Current Anthropology,* 7 (1966), 395–416.

2. Henry F. Dobyns, *Their Number Become Thinned: Native American Population Dynamics in Eastern North America* (Knoxville: University of Tennessee Press, 1983, p. 42.

3. The classic study here is Norma McArthur, *Island Populations in the Pacific* (Canberra: Australian National University Press, 1968). I should stress at this point that I am referring only to Pacific island populations. In recent years there have appeared several excellent reconsiderations of the pre-European Aboriginal population of Australia—reconsiderations founded on the American "Berkeley School" models that show vastly higher estimates in parts of Australia than previously imagined. See, for example, Dianne Kirkby, "Colonial Policy and Native Depopulation in California and New South Wales, 1770–1840," *Ethnohistory,* 31 (1984), 1–16; Noel Butlin, *Our Original Aggression: Aboriginal Populations of Southeastern Australia, 1788–1850* (Sydney: Allen & Unwin, 1983); and two recent articles on smallpox epidemics among Australian Aborigines by Butlin and Judy Campbell in *Historical Studies,* 21 (1985).

4. K. R. Howe, *The Loyalty Islands: A History of Culture Contacts, 1840–1900* (Honolulu: The University Press of Hawai'i, 1977), pp. x, 158; see also, K. R. Howe, "The Fate of the 'Savage' in Pacific Historiography," The *New Zealand Journal of History,* 11 (1977), 137–54. Howe's rhetoric is more overblown than most, but his assertion that massive depopulation did not occur following Western contact—despite his own evidence to the contrary—has now

become standard practice among students of Pacific history. The most recent example, as this book goes to press, is David Hanlon's *Upon A Stone Altar: A History of the Island of Pohnpei to 1890* (Honolulu: University of Hawaii Press, 1988). In the Preface to this otherwise excellent study Hanlon goes out of his way to describe the idea of large-scale depopulation in Pohnpei and elsewhere in the 18th and 19th century Pacific as "a grossly distorted, popular interpretation" that is completely at odds with reality (p. xvi). Then later, in passing, he notes nonchalantly that a *single* smallpox epidemic in 1854 reduced the native population of Pohnpei by more than *50 percent* (p. 204). Since this, like Howe's example, is a greater death rate than that experienced by the English during the Black Death, by Jews during the Holocaust, or by the Japanese residents of atomic-bombed Hiroshima and Nagasaki, one can only wonder how horrific a disaster must be for people like Hanlon and Howe to consider it significant.

5. Robert C. Schmitt, "New Estimates of the Pre-Censal Population of Hawai'i" *The Journal of the Polynesian Society*, 80 (1971), 240. For a convenient summary of earlier estimates, see Robert C. Schmitt, *Demographic Statistics of Hawai'i, 1778–1965* (Honolulu: University of Hawai'i Press, 1968), pp. 19–22. For information on McArthur's unfinished estimate I am grateful to her former colleague at Australian National University, Professor Gavan Daws, personal communication.

6. Francis Jennings, *The Invasion of America: Indians, Colonialism and the Cant of Conquest* (Chapel Hill: University of North Carolina Press, 1975), Chapter Two.

Chapter One

1. James King, "Journal," in J. C. Beaglehole, ed., *The Journals of Captain James Cook* (Cambridge: Hakluyt Society and the University Press, 1967), Volume III, Part One, p. 620.

2. James Cook, *The Three Voyages of Captain James Cook Round the World*, Volume VII by James King (London, 1821), pp. 118–119. This is a reprint of the same account rendered in *Captain Cook's Last Voyage to the Pacific Ocean* (London, 1793).

3. See Rupert T. Gould, "Some Unpublished Accounts of Cook's Death," *The Mariner's Mirror*, 14 (1928), 385.

4. Schmitt, "New Estimates," 238; Schmitt, *Demographic Statistics*, p. 21.

5. Schmitt, *Demographic Statistics*, p. 22.

6. Schmitt, "New Estimates," 240; *State of Hawai'i Data Book* (Honolulu: State Department of Planning and Economic Development, 1986), p. 64, and personal communication. Schmitt, "New Estimates," 237.

7. Schmitt, "New Estimates," 238; William M. Denevan, *The Native Population of the Americas in 1492* (Madison: University of Wisconsin Press, 1976), p. 7. For a similar observation on the relative magnitude of the Native American population collapse, see Wilbur R. Jacobs, "The Tip of the Iceberg: Pre-Columbian Indian Demography and Some Implications for Revisionism," *William and Mary Quarterly*, 3rd Series, 31 (1974), 123–32.

8. Dobyns, "Estimating Aboriginal American Population," 414–15, emphasis added. See also Sherburne F. Cook and Woodrow Borah, "On the Credibility of Contemporary Testimony of the Population of Mexico in the Sixteenth Century," in *Summa antropologica en homenaje a Roberto J. Weitlaner* (Mexico City: Instituto Nacional de Antropologia e Historia, 1966), pp. 229–39.

9. George Dixon, *A Voyage Round the World* (London: G. Goulding, 1789), pp. 267, 262, 252–53. On cutaneous tuberculosis and tuberculosis of the superficial lymph nodes, particularly in young people, see Edith M. Lincoln and Edward M. Sewell, *Tuberculosis in Children* (New York: McGraw-Hill, 1963), pp. 207–15 and 233–41; a concise recent discussion can be found in W. Christopher Duncan and Andrew H. Rudolf, "Tuberculosis and Atypical Mycobacterial Disorders," in Jeffrey P. Callen, ed., *Cutaneous Aspects of Internal Disease* (Chicago: Year Book Medical Publishers, 1981), pp. 343–59. On the impact of tuberculosis on Pacific island children, see Dubos and Waksman in Chapter 3, note 20. On newly-introduced diseases appearing in unfamiliar forms, see William H. McNeill, *Plagues and Peoples* (New York: Doubleday, 1976), p. 61. As for the medical consequences of drinking 'awa, it has been known for some time that heavy 'awa drinkers may develop, at most, a skin rash (and then only temporarily) as an allergic response—but its legendary disabling effects are still repeated uncritically as fact by many serious scholars of the Pacific. See Carl C. Pfeiffer, et al, "Effect of Kawa in Normal Subjects and Patients," in Daniel H. Efron, ed., *Ethnopharmacologic Search for Psychoactive Drugs* (Washington: U.S. Department of Health, Education, and Welfare, 1968), pp. 155–61; and F. Keller and M. W. Klohs, "A Review of the Chemistry and Pharmacology of the Constituents of *Piper Methysticum, Lloydia: A Quarterly Journal of Pharmocognosy and Allied Biological Sciences,* 26 (1963), 1–15. I am grateful to Dr. Richard Kekuni Blaisdell for bringing this material to my attention.

10. *Chapters on Hawai'i and the Marianas in V. M. Golvin's "Voyage Around the World . . . in the Years 1817, 1818, and 1819,"* translated by Ella Wiswell (Honolulu: Pacific Islands Program Miscellaneous Work Papers, 1974), p. 65. This is the edition of Golovnin used by Schmitt, so I am using it here as well. However, I should note that an expanded edition is now more conveniently available: V. M. Golovnin, *Around the World on the Kamchatka, 1817–1819,* translated by Ella L. Wiswell (Honolulu: University of Hawai'i Press, 1979).

11. Ibid., p. 59. Although it is apparent in the English translation that Golovnin was writing in the present tense, it is equally evident in the original Russian. I am grateful to Patricia Polansky, Russian Bibliographer for the University of Hawai'i Library, for confirming this for me.

12. Archibald Menzies, *Hawai'i Nei 128 Years Ago* (Honolulu: W. F. Wilson, 1920), p. 42.

13. Ibid., pp. 135–36, emphasis added.

14. A photostatic copy of Bayly's manuscript log and journal is in the Archives of Hawai'i, Cook Collection, item 185. Schmitt's citation indicates that he relied upon notes of Bayly's log and journal taken by the late historian of Hawai'i, Ralph S. Kuykendall.

15. William Ellis, *An Authentic Narrative of a Voyage* (London: G. Robinson,

1782), p. 149; John Rickman, *Journal of Captain Cook's Last Voyage* (London: E. Newberry, 1781), p. 226. Convenient summaries of Ni'ihau's current physiography, soil quality, and rainfall patterns are available in R. W. Armstrong, ed., *Atlas of Hawai'i*, 2nd Edition (Honolulu: University of Hawai'i Press, 1983), pp. 35–62.

16. Nathaniel Portlock, *Voyage Round the World* (London: Stockdale and Goulding, 1789), pp. 88, 90; see also William Henry Portlock, *A New, Complete, and Universal Collection of Authentic and Entertaining Voyages and Travels* (London: Alex. Hogg, 1794), p. 85.

17. Matthew Spriggs, " 'Preceded By Forest': Changing Interpretations of Landscape Change on Kaho'olawe," forthcoming.

18. See R. E. Dickenson, "Effects of Tropical Deforestation on Climate," *Studies in Third World Societies*, 14 (1981), 411–44; and A. Henderson Sellers, "The Effects of Land Clearance and Agricultural Practices on Climate," ibid., 443–85. On the comparison of Kaho'olawe with parts of the island of Hawai'i, see Spriggs, " 'Preceded By Forest.' " I have confirmed the matter of Kaho'olawe's drastically changed environment with hydrologist Catherine Vandemoer whose firm, Watershed Management Systems, is presently conducting a state contracted study of the island. "The evidence for a more abundant water resource in the past," she writes in a personal communication, "is demonstrated in the clay mineralogy of the island which shows that a considerable amount of leaching did occur, by stratigraphic evidence showing large quantities of soil and rock material transported downslope in the past, and by the size and number of gulches on the island." The fact that "water was a considerably more abundant resource on Kaho'olawe than is evidenced today" and the interactive relationship among water supply, vegetation, wind patterns—and back again to rainfall and water supply—will help "explain the large population concentration of Kaho'olawe and the role of the island within the larger cultural context of indigenous inhabitation of all the Hawaiian islands," writes Vandemoer. The quoted 19th century traveler is Isabella L. Bird, *Six Months in the Sandwich Islands* [1875] (Honolulu: University of Hawai'i Press, 1966), p. 133. Declining precipitation on the island of Hawai'i, especially acute in overgrazed areas of Kohala, is discussed in Robert D. Doty, "Annual Precipitation on the Island of Hawai'i between 1890 and 1977," *Pacific Science*, 36 (1982), 421–25. A striking photograph of the ghostly grid lines across part of the ancient and huge agricultural fields of now dry and barren Kohala on the island of Hawai'i appears in Patrick Vinton Kirch, *Feathered Gods and Fishhooks: An Introduction to Hawaiian Archaeology and Prehistory* (Honolulu: University of Hawai'i Press, 1985), p. 230.

19. Kenneth P. Emory, *The Island of Lāna'i: A Survey of Native Culture* (Honolulu: Bishop Museum Press, 1969—reprint of 1924 edition), p. 122; preceding quotations from pp. 7 and 50.

20. King, "Journal," p. 610; Emory, *Island of Lāna'i*, pp. 62–63; S. L. Washburn and Irven DeVore, "The Social Life of Baboons," *Scientific American*, 104 (1962), 62–71. Current, but as yet unpublished, archaeological research on Lāna'i supports my contention that Emory's estimate of the number of house sites was far too low and that (in archaeologist Matthew Spriggs's words, personal

communication) the island was indeed " 'fruitful and populous' even in the driest areas."

21. See, for example, C. S. Stewart, *Journal of a Residence in the Sandwich Islands During the Years 1823, 1824, and 1825* (London: Fisher & Jackson, 1830), p. 26. Like all estimates at this time, especially of the smaller and more remote islands, Stewart's figures are little more than second-hand reports of other peoples' guesses. It is in fact quite possible that the population of Lāna'i in the early 1820s—even after half a century of disastrous depopulation—was substantially higher than 3000. Note, for example, that soon after missionary William Patterson Alexander arrived on the Marquesan island of Nukuhiva in 1833—after a stay in Hawai'i—he wrote in his journal that "the population of the island I suppose is not greater than that of Lāna'i." It is fairly well established (as it was known at the time) that Nukuhiva then had a population at the very least of 6000 to 8000 people, and probably a good deal more. If Lāna'i did indeed contain this many people in the 1820s, it could easily have had three or four times that prior to 1778. Alexander's observation is noted in his journal letter to Hawai'i missionary Rufus Anderson of September 4, 1833 (Houghton Library, Harvard University) and is discussed in another context in T. Walter Herbert, Jr., *Marquesan Encounters: Melville and the Meaning of Civilization* (Cambridge: Harvard University Press, 1980), pp. 48–49. The population of Nukuhiva was estimated at 6000 to 8000 by various missionaries and a French naval officer in the early 1840s, when it was substantially less than it had been in the 1820s and 1830s. R. Thompson, "The Marquesas Islands: A Brief Account of Discovery and Early History," *London Missionary Society Journal* (1841); and L. Rollin, *Les îles Marquises* (Paris: Société d'éditions géographiques, maritimes et coloniales, 1929), p. 64. These and other contemporary 19th century population estimates of the various Marquesas Islands are summarized in McArthur, *Island Populations of the Pacific*, pp. 286–87, Table 54.

22. John Ledyard, *Journal of Captain Cook's Last Voyage* [1783], ed. J. K. Munford (Corvallis: Oregon State University Press, 1963), p. 103; Cook, "Journal," in Beaglehole, ed., *Journals of Captain James Cook*, Volume III, Part One, p. 491; David Samwell, "Some Account of a Voyage to the South Seas," in Beaglehole, ed., *Journals of Captain James Cook*, Volume III, Part Two, p. 1223.

23. The passage from Law's journal is quoted in Beaglehole, ed., *Journals of Captain James Cook*, Volume III, Part One, p. 592; Samwell, "Some Account of a Voyage," pp. 1175–76; Ledyard, *Journal of Captain Cook's Last Voyage*, p. 128; Christine Holmes, ed., *Captain Cook's Final Voyage: The Journal of Midshipman George Gilbert* (Sussex: Caliban Books, 1982), p. 101; Charles Clerke, "Journal," in Beaglehole, ed., *Journal of Captain James Cook*, Volume III, Part One, p. 593, emphasis added.

24. Cook, "Journal," p. 283; Samwell, "Some Account of a Voyage," p. 1176; Elisha Loomis, *Journal* (typescript copy in Hawai'i-Pacific Collection, University of Hawai'i Library), p. 8; King, *The Three Voyages of Captain James Cook*, Volume VII, p. 129; William Ellis, *Journal of William Ellis* [1825] (Rutland, Vermont: Charles E. Tuttle Company, 1979), p. 36; Paul H. Rosendahl, "Aboriginal Agriculture and Residence Patterns in Upland Lapakahi, Island of Hawai'i" (Doctoral

dissertation, University of Hawai'i, 1972) esp. pp. 240 ff. and 487; *The Missionary Herald* (October 1823), p. 315.

25. King, "Journal," p. 503; Rickman, *Journal*, p. 296; Ledyard, *Journal of Captain Cook's Last Voyage*, p. 103.

26. Daniel Tyerman and George Bennet, *Journal of Voyages and Travels*, James Montgomery, compiler (Boston: Crocker and Brewster, 1852), Volume II, pp. 15–16; Ellis, *Journal of William Ellis*, pp. 29, 36, 76. I am grateful to University of Hawai'i cartographer Everett A. Wingert for calculating for me the precise distance between Keauhou and Kailua, which is substantially less than Ellis supposed.

27. See the discussions by T. Stell Newman, *Hawaiian Fishing and Farming on the Island of Hawai'i in A.D. 1778* (Honolulu: State of Hawai'i Department of Land and Natural Resources, 1970); and Marion Kelly, *Nā Māla o Kona: Gardens of Kona, A History of Land Use in Kona, Hawai'i* (Honolulu: Bishop Museum Dept. of Anthropology Report 83-2, 1983). On the quality of water during Cook's visit, see Ledyard, *Journal of Captain Cook's Last Voyage*, pp. 139, 155. In addition to Kealakekua on Hawai'i and Waimea on Kaua'i, King did spend a small part of one rainy afternoon on the beach at Waimea on O'ahu (noting that it was very well cultivated, highly populated—although most of the men of the area were then absent—and exceptionally beautiful), but circumstances forced the ships to depart before nightfall.

28. Charles Clerke, "Journal," p. 591; King, "Journal," pp. 605–06; Cook, "Journal," p. 501; Samwell, "Some Account of a Voyage," p. 1152, 1156; Ellis, *An Authentic Narrative of a Voyage*, p. 149; Holmes, ed., *Captain Cook's Final Voyage*, p. 100; Rickman, *Journal*, p. 296. On the limited archaeological work that has thus far been conducted in the northern valleys of the island of Hawai'i, see H. D. Tuggle and M. J. Tomonari-Tuggle, "Prehistoric Agriculture in Kohala, Hawai'i," *Journal of Field Archaeology*, 7(1980), 297–312.

29. T. K. Earle, "Prehistoric Irrigation in the Hawaiian Islands: An Evaluation of Evolutionary Significance," *Archaeology and Physical Anthropology in Oceania*, 15 (1980), 1–28.

30. R. P. D. Walsh, "The Nature of Climatic Seasonality," in Robert Chambers, Richard Longhurst, and Arnold Pacey, eds., *Seasonal Dimensions to Rural Poverty* (London: Allanheld & Osmun, 1981), p. 16. In Hawai'i, see W. T. Nakamura, "A Study in the Variation in Annual Rainfall of O'ahu Island," *Monthly Weather Review*, 61 (1933), 354–60; and J. C. Ripperton and E. Y. Hosaka, "Vegetation Zones of Hawai'i," *Agricultural Experiment Station Bulletin*, No. 89 (University of Hawai'i, 1942), pp. 10–11.

31. Robert J. Hommon, "The Formation of Primitive States in Pre-Contact Hawai'i" (Doctoral dissertation, University of Arizona, 1976), p. 36.

32. T. Stell Newman, "Man in the Prehistoric Hawaiian Ecosystem," in E. Allison Kay, ed., *A Natural History of the Hawaiian Islands* (Honolulu: University Press of Hawai'i, 1972), p. 587.

33. Marion Kelly, "Dynamics of Production Intensification in Pre-Contact Hawai'i," in S. van der Leeuw and R. Torrence, eds., *What's New? A Closer Look at the Process of Innovation* (London: Unwin Hyman, forthcoming). Emphasis added.

34. Samuel M. Kamakau, *Ruling Chiefs of Hawai'i* (Honolulu: Kamehameha Schools Press, 1961), p. 63. Dobyns, *Their Number Become Thinned*, pp. 174–89.

35. I am again grateful to Everett A. Wingert for calculating for me the coastal mileage of each of the island of Hawai'i's ancient districts.

36. Samwell, "Some Account of a Voyage," p. 1221; Clerke, "Journal," pp. 572–73; William K. Kikuchi, "Hawaiian Aquacultural Systems" (Doctoral dissertation, University of Arizona, 1973); Kelly, "Dynamics of Production Intensification."

37. J. F. G. de la Pérouse, *A Voyage Round the World* (London: A. Hamilton, 1799), Volume I, p. 352.

38. King, "Journal," p. 606; and King, *Captain Cook's Last Voyage to the Pacific Ocean*, p. 677. See also the description by the *Discovery*'s Captain Charles Clerke in ibid., p. 591.

39. Personal communication with Joseph Kennedy and Bertel Davis, archaeologists who have done—and continue to do—extensive work in the 'Ewa district of O'ahu.

40. See, among many sources, Marion Kelly, *Majestic Ka'ū: Mo'olelo of Nine Ahupua'a* (Honolulu: Bishop Museum Dept. of Anthropology Report 80-2, 1980), pp. 10, 22–33; William M. Barrera, Jr. and Robert Hommon, *Salvage Archaeology at Wailau, Ka'ū, Island of Hawai'i* (Honolulu: Bishop Museum Dept. of Anthropology Report 72-1, 1972), p. 33; and Kenneth P. Emory, *Inventory of Archaeological and Historical Sites in the Districts of Kona and Ka'ū and in 'Anaeho'omalu, South Kohala, Island of Hawai'i* (Honolulu: Bishop Museum Dept. of Anthropology Report 70-12, 1970).

41. Cook, "Journal," p. 486.

42. King, "Journal," p. 607.

43. On Romer's Rule see Elman R. Service, *Cultural Evolutionism: Theory in Practice* (New York: Holt, Rinehart and Winston, 1971), p. 12. For discussion see Catherine H. Maserang, "Factors Affecting Carrying Capacities of Nation-States," *Journal of Anthropological Research*, 32 (1976), 268; and Catherine Hodge McCoid, *Carrying Capacities of Nation-States* (New Haven: Human Relations Area Files, 1984), p. 119.

44. For archaeological comments see, for example, David O. Denison and Arthur S. Forman, *Archaeological Investigations in South Hālawa Valley, 'Ewa District, Island of O'ahu—Phase II* (Honolulu: Bishop Museum Dept. of Anthropology Report 71-9, 1971). The ongoing work in O'ahu's Anahulu Valley provides another well-known example. On the *mauka/makai* economic patterns see the discussion in E. S. Craighill Handy and Mary Kawena Pukui, *The Polynesian Family System in Ka'ū, Hawai'i* (Rutland, Vermont: Charles E. Tuttle, 1972), Chapter I.

45. Cook, "Journal," p. 487.

46. Menzies, *Hawai'i Nei 128 Years Ago*, p. 185. The descriptive language in the sentence preceding this quotation is from Menzies, ibid., and from Handy and Pukui, *Polynesian Family System*, p. 226.

47. Menzies, *Hawai'i Nei*, pp. 185–86.

48. On this and related matters see Kelly, *Majestic Ka'ū*, pp. 43-50.

49. Denison and Forman, *Archaeological Investigations in South Hālawa Valley*, p. 59, emphasis in original. On the inland population of New Zealand (Aoteora) and the failure of early explorers to take account of it, see Te Rangihiroa, "The Passing of the Maori," *Transactions and Proceedings of the New Zealand Institute*, 55 (1924), 363-64; Gordon Lewthwaite, "The Population of Aotearoa: Its Number and Distribution," *New Zealand Geographer*, 6 (1950), 36-39, 44; and D. Ian Pool, *The Maori Population of New Zealand, 1769-1971* (Auckland: Auckland University Press, 1977), pp. 50-51.

50. According to the *Atlas of Hawai'i*, p. 219, the total coastline of Hawai'i, Maui, Kaho'olawe, Lāna'i, Moloka'i, O'ahu, Kaua'i and Ni'ihau is 797 miles.

51. To achieve the lowest possible depopulation rate, I chose Schmitt's midpoint estimate for 1778 of 225,000 and the conventional estimate for 1823 of about 140,000. For discussion of this latter figure, see Schmitt, *Demographic Statistics*, pp. 24-25.

Chapter Two

1. Because most archaeology in Hawai'i is now so-called "contract" archaeology, funded by private corporations or state agencies, it is very slow in getting to press. In addition, the expense of carbon dating has precluded the evaluation of a great deal of data; the anthropology department of Honolulu's Bishop Museum, for example, has approximately 600 Hawaiian site samples that have never been dated (more than twice the number that have been dated) because of the financial costs involved. However, recently uncovered evidence of sites inhabited no later than the first century A.D.—and possibly much earlier—is discussed in Patricia Beggerly, "Artifactual Landscape: Kahana Valley, O'ahu, Hawai'i," *Hawaiian Archaeology*, 2 (forthcoming) and the as yet unpublished report by J. E. Bath and Paul Rosendahl, "Subsurface Archaeological Reconnaissance Survey, Kuilima Resort Expansion Project." In addition, personal communications with archaeologists working in Hawai'i—Matthew Spriggs, Tom Dye, and others—report equally early radiocarbon datings in other parts of the island, including leeward O'ahu. Indeed, the growing evidence of such early human settlement has already begun to generate wholesale reappraisals of early Polynesian history, such as Patrick V. Kirch's "Rethinking East Polynesian Prehistory," *Journal of the Polynesian Society*, 95 (1986), 9-40. The computer simulations showing that Hawai'i had to have been settled intentionally are reported in M. Levison, R. G. Ward, and J. W. Webb, *The Settlement of Polynesia: A Computer Simulation* (Minneapolis: University of Minnesota Press, 1973).

2. David Lewis, *We, the Navigators: The Ancient Art of Landfinding in the Pacific* (Honolulu: University of Hawai'i Press, 1972), pp. 274-75; Samwell, "Some Account of a Voyage," p. 1184.

3. Norma McArthur, I. W. Saunders, and R. L. Tweedie, "Small Population Isolates: A Micro-Simulation Study," *Journal of the Polynesian Society*, 85 (1976), 307-26. For some notable earlier efforts, see J. Sutter and L. Tabah, "Les

notions d'isolat et de population minimum," *Population,* 6 (1951), 481–98; and R. B. Lee and Irven DeVore, *Man the Hunter* (Chicago: Aldine, 1968), p. 245. On Pitcairn, see Patrick Vinton Kirch, *The Evolution of the Polynesian Chiefdoms* (Cambridge: Cambridge University Press, 1984), p. 96; and J. B. Birdsell, "Some Population Problems Involving Pleistocene Man," *Cold Spring Harbor Symposia on Quantitative Biology,* 22 (1957), 68.

4. See the convenient table and discussion in Paul R. Ehrlich, Anne H. Ehrlich, and John P. Holdren, *Ecoscience: Population, Resources, Environment* (San Francisco: W. H. Freeman and Company, 1977), pp. 208–09. For contemporary Third World population data, see Population Reference Bureau, *1986 World Population Data Sheet* (Washington, D.C., 1987).

5. McArthur, et al, "Small Population Isolates," 309–10.

6. Ibid., 317.

7. Ibid., 318.

8. Robert J. Hommon, "Social Evolution in Ancient Hawai'i" in P. V. Kirch, ed., *Island Societies: Archaeological Approaches to Evolution and Transformation* (Cambridge: Cambridge University Press, 1986), p. 60. Fekri A. Hassan, *Demographic Archaeology* (New York: Academic Press, 1981), p. 140. Robert C. Schmitt and Lynn Y. S. Zane, *How Many People Have Ever Lived in Hawaii?* (Honolulu: Hawai'i Department of Planning and Economic Development, 1977).

9. A good discussion of health and mortality conditions in England between the 15th and 17th centuries can be found in Paul Slack, "Mortality Crises and Epidemic Disease in England, 1485–1610," in Charles Webster, ed., *Health, Medicine, and Mortality in the Sixteenth Century* (Cambridge: Cambridge University Press, 1979), pp. 9–59. Among the many accounts of Irish population and social conditions between 1750 and 1850 (which saw the population more than double despite the great starvation and outmigration) see especially Cecil Woodham-Smith, *The Great Hunger* (London: Hamish-Hamilton, 1962).

10. On South Point on the island of Hawai'i, see the discussion in Patrick Vinton Kirch, *Feathered Gods and Fishhooks,* pp. 81–87; on Kaua'i see A. Rose Schilt, "Archaeological Investigations in Specified Areas of the Hanalei Wildlife Refuge, Hanalei Valley, Kaua'i" (typescript in Bishop Museum Library, Honolulu, 1980); on Moloka'i see Patrick V. Kirch and Marion Kelly, eds., *Prehistory and Ecology in a Windward Hawaiian Valley: Hālawa Valley, Moloka'i* (Honolulu: Bishop Museum Press, 1975); and on Maui see Kenneth P. Emory, *An Archaeological Survey of Haleakalā* (Honolulu: Bishop Museum Occasional Papers, 1921) and the evidence of dating possibly as early as the 7th century in Lloyd Soehren, "An Archaeological Survey of Portions of East Maui, Hawai'i" (report in Bishop Museum Library, Honolulu, 1963). This does not, of course, exhaust the list of sites dating to this early period nor the number of reports on any of them; it merely is meant to illustrate the geographic range of such early sites.

11. Robert E. Dewar, "Environmental Productivity, Population Regulation, and Carrying Capacity," *American Anthropologist,* 86 (1984), 601; for an earlier critique of the concept see Brian Hayden, "The Carrying Capacity Dilemma: An Alternate Approach," *American Antiquity,* 40 (1975), Number 2, Part 2, 11–21.

12. See the discussion in Barbara Pickersgill and Richard T. Smith, "Adaptation to a Desert Coast: Subsistence Changes Through Time in Coastal Peru," in Don Brothwell and Geoffrey Dimbleby, eds., *Environmental Aspects of Coasts and Islands* (Oxford: British Archaeological Reports International Series 94, 1981), pp. 89–115.

13. Noble David Cook, *Demographic Collapse: Indian Peru, 1520–1620* (Cambridge: Cambridge University Press, 1981), p. 37.

14. Ibid., p. 108. Other estimates have been both higher and lower, but Cook's is the most detailed and careful analysis to date.

15. Among many discussions, see especially Paula Brown, *Highland Peoples of New Guinea* (Cambridge: Cambridge University Press, 1978), Chapter 2; and Hassan, *Demographic Archaeology*, esp. Chapter 4. Hassan in particular draws on the important synthesis by Marshall Sahlins in *Stone Age Economics* (Chicago: Aldine-Atherton, 1972).

16. See the excellent summary in Robert S. Santley, Thomas W. Killion, and Mark T. Lycett, "On the Maya Collapse," *Journal of Anthropological Research*, 42 (1986), 123–59.

17. For Hispaniola see Sherburne F. Cook and Woodrow Borah, "The Aboriginal Population of Hispaniola," in their *Essays in Population History: Mexico and the Caribbean* (Berkeley: University of California Press, 1971), Volume I, pp. 376–410; on Tapituea see Brothwell and Dimbleby, eds., *Environmental Aspects of Coasts and Islands*, pp. 2–3. On Banaba Island, see H. C. Maude and H. E. Maude, "The Social Organization of Banaba or Ocean Island, Central Pacific," *Journal of the Polynesian Society*, 41 (1932), 262–301. On the Polynesian Outlier atolls, see Tim Bayliss-Smith, "Constraints on Population Growth: The Case of the Polynesian Outlier Atolls in the Precontact Period," *Human Ecology*, 2 (1974), 287–88; and Edward E. Hunt, Jr., Nathaniel R. Kidder, and David M. Schneider, "The Depopulation of Yap," *Human Biology*, 26 (1954), 22. Although it commonly is assumed that smaller coral islands can sustain far greater population densities than high volcanic islands, this is a subject that deserves much more study. While it is true that intensive taro cultivation is possible in the centers of such smaller islands, overall their cultivable land areas are extremely limited and population sustenance is heavily dependent on ocean resources.

18. See Kelly, "Dynamics of Production Intensification."

19. W. Gordon East, *The Geography Behind History*, Revised Edition (New York: W. W. Norton & Company, 1965), pp. 52–53; Fernand Braudel, *Capitalism and Material Life, 1400–1800* (New York: Harper & Row), 1973, pp. 43, 82. A classic essay is M. Postan's "Some Economic Evidence of Declining Population in the Later Middle Ages," *Economic History Review*, 2nd Series, 2 (1950), 221–46.

20. On the plague see Josiah C. Russell, "Late Ancient and Medieval Population," *American Philosophical Society Transactions*, 48 (1958), 40–45; Philip Ziegler, *The Black Death* (New York: Harper & Row, 1969), pp. 224 ff.; and McNeill, *Plagues and Peoples*, pp. 166–69. For the conservative estimated population density of late 14th century England see B. H. Slicher Van Bath, *The Agrarian History of Western Europe, A.D. 500–1850* (New York: Saint Martin's Press, 1963), p. 81. He is relying on the 19th century calculations of J. Baloch.

For Duby's discussion of the underenumeration, see his *Rural Economy and Country Life in the Medieval West*, translated by Cynthia Postan (London: Edward Arnold, Ltd., 1968), p. 299. On ancient Sumer—as well as a summary of other non-urban estimates, including 5000 per square mile in parts of north-central Java—see Eric R. Wolf, *Peasants* (Englewood Cliffs, New Jersey: Prentice-Hall, 1966), pp. 24-29. As for the reference to Hawai'i's "nearly disease-free people," one reader of an early draft of this piece questioned this description in light of current estimates of pre-*haole* Hawaiian life expectancies of around 30 to 32 years (about the same as 18th century European life expectancies). The diseases I am referring to, of course, are infectious diseases of epidemic potential—and such do not appear to have existed in pre-*haole* Hawai'i for reasons that I explore in a separate forthcoming essay; for the present it must suffice to note that the paleopathological study of pre-*haole* Hawaiian remains shows no evidence of such disease, a fact that is predictable in light of the great length of time that Hawaiians lived in virtual isolation from the rest of the world. On the beneficent influence of such isolation, see the succinct comments of René Dubos in his *Man, Medicine, and Environment* (London: Pall Mall Press, 1971), pp. 68-71. As for the pre-*haole* life expectancy of Hawaiians, it almost certainly was much greater than is now conventionally believed. The scientific basis for making such estimates recently has been shown to have major deficiencies that bias life expectancy estimates of indigenous peoples unreasonably downward. Even subsequent defenders of such paleodemographic techniques now admit that age estimates of older adults in such populations are almost invariably far too low. See Jean-Pierre Bocquet-Appel and Claude Masset, "Farewell to Paleodemography," *Journal of Human Evolution*, 11 (1982), 321-33 and the reply by Jane E. Buikstra and Lyle W. Konigsberg, "Paleodemography: Critiques and Controversies," *American Anthropologist*, 87 (1985), 316-33.

21. For the pre-Western populations and densities of the Mangareva (or Gambier) Islands and Rapanui, see Kirch, *Evolution of the Polynesian Chiefdoms*, p. 19; Kirch acknowledges, however, that the stated population for Rapanui, which produces a density of over 109 people per square mile (the equivalent in Hawai'i of over 700,000 people) on that relatively inhospitable island "may be an underestimate" (p. 271). For the pre-European population densities of Tahiti and the Marquesas (between 107 and 127 people per square mile in Tahiti and as many as 200 per square mile in the Marquesas) I have based my computations on the pre-*haole* population estimates of the outstanding non-native historians of these islands, Douglas L. Oliver, in his *Ancient Tahitian Society*, 3 Volumes (Honolulu: University Press of Hawai'i, 1974) and Greg Dening in *Islands and Beaches—Discourse on a Silent Land: Marquesas, 1774-1880* (Honolulu: University Press of Hawai'i, 1980). However, a word must be said about Oliver's figures. In what appears to be a last-minute footnote added to the opening section of his massive study, Oliver says he can "only echo" Norma McArthur's extremely low estimate of about 35,000 for the pre-*haole* population of Tahiti. (Estimates at the time of contact ranged up to Captain Cook's 204,000.) However, in other places (e.g., pp. 966, 968) Oliver says that the 1797 population of Tahiti (which he and McArthur put at between 16,000 and 19,000—following the contemporary estimate of

William Wilson) was "by conservative estimate . . . about a quarter of its previous size." This yields a pre-*haole* figure ranging—"by conservative estimate"—from 64,000 to about 76,000. Moreover, Oliver later accepts a figure for the late 1780s and early 1790s of 30,000 provided by James Morrison, one of the *Bounty*'s mutineers who lived in Tahiti from October of 1778 to April of 1791. If accurate, that would mean the population dropped by almost half between the late 1780s and the late 1790s—from 30,000 to between 16,000 and 19,000—presumably at least in part the result of an epidemic of "bloody flux" traceable to George Vancouver's 1791–92 expedition. We also know, however, that Tahiti was ravaged by disease prior to Morrison's estimate of 30,000; in addition to venereal disease and probably tuberculosis, Tahiti was devastated by a disease apparently brought by Captain Cook's crews that, Cook observed on his 1773 return voyage, "affects the head, throat, and stomack and at length kills them" (Beaglehole, *Journals of Captain James Cook*, Volume II, pp. 231–32). And, of course, Cook's first visit to Tahiti was preceded by those of Captains Samuel Wallis and Louis Antoine de Bougainville. Wallis's crew, and Wallis himself, were desperately sick for much of their voyage up to and during their arrival in Tahiti. They were, predictably, badly afflicted with scurvy, but also with other vaguely-described infections such as "a bilious cholic." In addition, a number of the crew (probably at least twenty) began the voyage with venereal disease; the fact that the ship's surgeon later claimed that no one aboard was *visibly* affected with it when they went ashore in Tahiti says nothing about the possibility—indeed, the virtual certainty—of contagion, since remission and not cure was the best that could then be hoped for in the treatment of V.D. Although Bougainville's crew almost certainly also brought such infections to Tahiti, when Cook arrived there on only the second English voyage to the islands, he found the Tahitians referring to venereal disease as "apa no pretane" or "English disease." [See George Robertson, *The Discovery of Tahiti: A Journal*, ed., Hugh Carrington (London: Hakluyt Society, 1948), pp. 284–87.] As we shall see later, an extremely rapid population decline commencing almost immediately upon contact with the West would be consistent with other "first contact" situations. It is thus probable that Oliver's—and others'—"conservative estimate" producing a pre-*haole* figure of at least 64,000 to 76,000 (about 107 to 127 per square mile) is in fact a modest approximation of reality. This is not the place to scrutinize in detail McArthur's highly misleading estimates (though some day that shall have to be done), but some of her gaffes and her fundamental error of, in Peter Pirie's words, "discount[ing] any figures which do not appear to have been carefully gathered and tabulated with census-like accuracy" are discussed in Pirie's excellent critique of her book in *Australian Geographical Studies*, 6 (1968), 175–81. Since such "census-like" tabulations invariably were carried out long after the first waves of the European bacteriological invasion had turned the islands, like the American Indians' homelands, into "widowed lands," McArthur's estimates just as invariably ignore the devastating effects of disease on indigenous populations in the years immediately following first contact. Apart from its exposure in the pioneering work of Borah and Cook, precisely this common failing among early writers was demonstrated and corrected in some detail, using the Andes as a case study, five years before McArthur's major work was published—

so it is hardly unfair to expect her to have been aware of it; see Henry F. Dobyns, "An Outline of Andean Epidemic History to 1720," *Bulletin of the History of Medicine*, 37 (1963), 493–515. It is ironic, however, that the one time McArthur did a truly detailed analysis of an island population (her doctoral dissertation on the island of Aneityum), she provided the foundation for a subsequent analysis which showed that tiny island to have had, conservatively, a pre-Western population density of up to 94 people per square mile and a subsequent population collapse of about 97 percent within a century following Western contact! See Matthew J. Spriggs, "Vegetable Kingdoms: Taro Irrigation and Pacific Prehistory" (Doctoral dissertation, Austrialian National University, 1981), esp. Chapter 4.

22. Population densities for these rural areas on Kaua'i and O'ahu were computed from the tables on land area and resident population in *The State of Hawai'i Data Book* (Honolulu: Hawai'i Department of Planning and Economic Development, 1987). On the Nā Pali valleys see Myra J. Tomonari-Tuggle, *An Archaeological Reconnaissance Survey: Nā Pali Coast State Park, Island of Kaua'i* (Honolulu: State Department of Land and Natural Resources, 1979).

23. William Shaler, *Journal of a Voyage Between China and the Northwestern Coast of America* (Philadelphia, 1808), p. 112; Campbell, *A Voyage Round The World*, pp. 140–42; Clerke, "Journal," p. 592; Samwell, "Some Account of a Voyage," p. 1184; Menzies, *Hawai'i Nei 128 Years Ago*, p. 105.

24. See Robert C. Schmitt, *The Missionary Censuses of Hawai'i* (Honolulu: Bishop Museum Press, 1973), p. 8; and Schmitt, *Demographic Statistics of Hawai'i*, p. 74.

25. Cook and Borah, "Aboriginal Population of Hispaniola," p. 401.

26. Cook, *Demographic Collapse*, p. 114, emphasis added.

27. W. George Lovell, *Conquest and Survival in Colonial Guatemala: A Historical Geography of the Cuchumatan Highlands, 1500–1821* (Montreal: McGill-Queen's University Press, 1985), p. 145.

28. McNeill, *Plagues and Peoples*, p. 204.

29. Russell Thornton, "Social Organization and the Demographic Survival of the Tolowa," *Ethnohistory*, 31 (1984), 191–92.

30. Sherburne F. Cook, "The Extent and Significance of Disease Among the Indians of Baja California, 1697–1773," *Ibero-Americana*, 12 (1937).

31. David R. Radell, "The Indian Slave Trade and Population of Nicaragua During the Sixteenth Century," in Denevan, ed., *The Native Population of the Americas*, pp. 67–76.

32. John Hemming, *Red Gold: The Conquest of the Brazilian Indians, 1500–1760* (Cambridge: Harvard University Press, 1978), p. 492.

33. Dobyns, *Their Number Become Thinned*, p. 287.

34. E. Wagner and Allan E. Stearn, *The Effect of Smallpox on the Destiny of the Amerindian* (Boston: Bruce Humphries, 1945), p. 14.

35. René Dubos, *Man Adapting* (New Haven: Yale University Press, 1965), p. 173.

36. James Axtell, *The Invasion Within: The Contest of Cultures in Colonial North America* (New York: Oxford University Press, 1985), pp. 219–20, for the

Patuxet and Massachusett examples and for the overall pre-European population; for the post-European numbers see Sherburne F. Cook, "The Significance of Disease in the Extinction of the New England Indians," *Human Biology*, 45 (1973), 485–508. Although in this piece Cook used the low pre-European figures first proposed by James Mooney and John R. Swanton, by the time the study was published he had become convinced that the correct figure "was far greater than has been indicated." He then added, in words equally appropriate to Hawai'i and the Pacific: "The same old story." See Wilbur R. Jacobs, "Sherburne Friend Cook: Rebel-Revisionist (1896–1974)," *Pacific Historical Review*, 54 (1985), 191.

37. Sherburne F. Cook and Woodrow Borah, *The Indian Population of Central Mexico, 1531–1610*, Ibero-Americana, No. 44 (Berkeley: University of California Press, 1960); and Woodrow Borah and Sherburne F. Cook, *The Aboriginal Population of Central Mexico on the Eve of the Spanish Conquest*, Ibero-Americana, No. 45 (Berkeley: University of California Press, 1963).

38. Clinton R. Edwards, "Quintana Roo: Mexico's Empty Quarter" (Master's thesis, University of California at Berkeley, 1957), pp. 128, 132.

39. Butlin, *Our Original Aggression*, p. 147.

40. I am basing these numbers on the conventionally accepted populations of about 200,000 in 1769, about 85,000 in 1840, and about 48,000 by the early 1870s. See Lewthwaite, "The Population of Aotearoa," 32–52; and Pool, *The Maori Population of New Zealand*, pp. 195–96. Although not yet in print, I am told by University of Auckland Maori scholar Pat Hohepa that the most recent acceptable figure for 1769 is "at least half a million," a figure that is also mentioned by Pool (p. 24) and one that would, of course, make the decline much worse. In the interests of caution, however, I am not using that figure here. On the matter of late colonization and the benefits of vaccination, as well as a good general discussion of the ecological and epidemiological impact of the West on the traditional world of the Maori, see Alfred W. Crosby, *Ecological Imperialism: The Biological Expansion of Europe, 900–1900* (Cambridge: Cambridge University Press, 1986), pp. 217–68.

41. Dening, *Islands and Beaches*, p. 239; the nadir population figure is for 1902 —104 years after contact—from C. Valenziani, cited in McArthur, *Island Populations of the Pacific*, p. 287

42. Spriggs, "Vegetable Kingdoms," Chapter 4; the nadir figure is from Norma McArthur, " 'And, Behold, the Plague Was Begun Among the People,' " in Neil Gunson, ed., *The Changing Pacific* (Melbourne: Oxford University Press, 1978), p. 282.

43. See McArthur, *Island Populations of the Pacific*, pp. 296 ff.; and Donald Marshall, *Raivavae* (New York: Doubleday, 1961), pp. 39–40.

44. See discussion in note 21, above. The population in 1829—62 years after contact—is taken from J. Davies's count, cited in McArthur, *Island Populations of the Pacific*, p. 261.

45. Ibid., pp. 167–74. See also Raeburn Lange, "Plagues and Pestilence in Polynesia: The Nineteenth-Century Cook Islands Experience," *Bulletin of the History of Medicine*, 58 (1984), esp. 346.

46. For the pre-European populations see Kirch, *Evolution of the Polynesian*

Chiefdoms, p. 19; for the nadir population of Easter Island see ibid., p. 264; for the Mangareva nadir see McArthur, *Island Populations of the Pacific,* p. 313.

47. Anastasia M. Shkilnyk, *A Poison Stronger than Love: The Destruction of an Ojibwa Community,* Foreword by Kai Erikson (New Haven: Yale University Press, 1985), p. xiv; McNeill, *Plagues and Peoples,* p. 205.

48. William A. Starna, "Mohawk Iroquois Population: A Revision," *Ethnohistory,* 27 (1980), 376-77.

49. Dobyns, "Estimating Aboriginal American Population," 412-14; McNeill, *Plagues and Peoples,* p. 215; Dobyns, *Their Number Become Thinned,* p. 343. On coastal populations see, for example, Borah and Cook's summary for the coasts of Mexico (a depopulation ratio of 47.8 to 1—or 98 percent—in half a century) in "Conquest and Population: A Demographic Approach to Mexican History," *Proceedings of the American Philosophical Society,* 113 (1969), 181. See also the same authors' discussion in "The Historical Demography of Interior Tribes of Columbia in the Studies of Juan Friede and German Colmenares," *Essays in Population History,* Volume I, pp. 411-29 and p. xiii; and their "On the Credibility of Contemporary Testimony," pp. 235-36.

50. Among numerous citations see, for example, the 1786 comments of Captain Pérouse and his surgeon finding "most" and "the greater part of" the Hawaiians ravaged by "the most destructive [scourges] with which the human race are afflicted." Captain George Vancouver, who had been with Cook during the 1778-79 trips to Hawai'i, was struck by the difference between the "numerous throngs" of people he had seen during the first voyage and the "very few" he saw in 1792—including a depletion by "at least two-thirds" of the population of Waimea on Kaua'i. Ignorant of the terrible destructiveness of the diseases that first visit had brought to Hawai'i, but acknowledging that in the fourteen years since the time of the first voyage "the mortality must have been very considerable," Vancouver assumed the deaths to have been caused primarily by war; but, as he admitted, the brevity of his second visit and the problem of language prevented him from ascertaining the actual cause of the great decline. (There were wars during this time, but, as Schmitt has pointed out, the death rate from them was relatively small compared with disease; the highest estimate of death caused by war up to 1796 is about 18,000 people, including those who died as a secondary consequence of war and its depredations—but this figure has long been correctly criticized for being far too large.) See Pérouse, *A Voyage Round the World,* Volume I, p. 348 and Volume II, pp. 337-38; George Vancouver, *A Voyage of Discovery . . . Round the World* (London, 1798), Volume I, pp. 158, 187-88; Robert C. Schmitt, "Catastrophic Mortality in Hawaii," *Hawaiian Journal of History,* 3 (1969), 66-67; and Robert C. Schmitt, "Famine Mortality in Hawai'i," *The Journal of Pacific History,* 5 (1970), 110.

51. R. C. Wyllie, *Answers to Questions Proposed by His Excellency* (Honolulu: Department of Foreign Affairs, 1848), pp. 20, 49, 52, 60, 95. The best source for death/birth ratios, which in some districts reached levels of 3 and 4 to 1 during the 1840s, are the annual Mission Station Reports on file at the Hawaiian Mission Children's Society Library in Honolulu.

52. Ibid., p. 60.

53. Ibid., p. 25.
54. Ellis, *Journal of William Ellis*, p. 223.
55. See the table in Schmitt, *Demographic Statistics*, p. 42.
56. On the 'ōku'u see Robert C. Schmitt, "The 'Ōku'u—Hawai'i's Greatest Epidemic," *Hawaii Medical Journal*, 29 (1970), 359–64. Schmitt estimates that the epidemic killed about 15,000 people; other estimates are much higher. In an unpublished manuscript entitled "The Sliding Way of Death," microbiologist O. A. Bushnell reviews the medical symptoms recorded in the historical literature and concludes that the disease was probably typhoid fever. Coincidentally, perhaps, there was a typhoid epidemic in London, a major shipping point to Hawai'i, just two years earlier. On the London epidemic, see the classic study by Charles Creighton, *A History of Epidemics in Britain* (Cambridge: Cambridge University Press, 1894), Volume II, pp. 159–61.
57. Tyerman and Bennet, *Journal of Voyages and Travels*, p. 35; Kamakau, *Ruling Chiefs*, p. 236; Levi Chamberlain, *Journal* (entry for May 21, 1826), on file at Hawaiian Mission Children's Society Library, Honolulu.
58. Isaac Bliss, Mission Station Report from District of Kohala (1844) on file at Hawaiian Mission Children's Society Library, Honolulu.
59. David Malo, "On the Decrease of Population in the Hawaiian Islands," *Hawaiian Spectator*, April 1839, p. 125; *Missionary Herald*, December 1829, p. 371—also cited in Schmitt, *Demographic Statistics*, p. 36.

Chapter Three

1. Eleanor C. Nordyke, *The Peopling of Hawai'i* (Honolulu: University Press of Hawai'i, 1977), p. 10.
2. O. A. Bushnell, "Hygiene and Sanitation Among the Ancient Hawaiians," *Hawai'i Historical Review*, 2 (1966); more conveniently available in Richard A. Greer, ed., *Hawai'i Historical Review: Selected Readings* (Honolulu: Hawaiian Historical Society, 1969), pp. 13–36; King, *The Three Voyages of Captain James Cook*, Volume VII, pp. 130–31; and Archibald Campbell, *A Voyage Round the World* (New York, 1817), pp. 121, 130–31.
3. For a convenient discussion of pre-*haole* Hawaiian food and nutrition, see Carey D. Miller, "The Influence of Foods and Food Habits Upon the Stature and Teeth of the Ancient Hawaiians," in Charles E. Snow, *Early Hawaiians: An Initial Study of Skeletal Remains from Mōkapu, O'ahu* (Lexington: The University Press of Kentucky, 1974), pp. 167–75. A recent and still unpublished study comparing the observed effects of traditional Hawaiian and modern American diets has found the typical American diet to contain (in addition to excessive sodium) at least four times the total fat, saturated fat, and cholesterol—and more than five times the sugar—than the traditional Hawaiian diet. These are, of course, nutrients closely associated with obesity, atherosclerosis (as in heart attack and stroke), diabetes, and hypertension. And, in fact, subjects placed on the two diets evidenced dramatically lower blood cholesterol and blood triglyceride values on the traditional Hawaiian diet than on the modern American diet. Preliminary data on the study's results have been discussed by Kekuni Blaisdell, M.D., in the

Office of Hawaiian Affairs publication, *Ka Wai Ola O OHA* (April and August 1988). On the Hawaiians' abilities to heal bone fractures, see Walter F. Bowers, "Pathological and Functional Changes Found in 864 Pre-Captain Cook Contact Polynesian Burials From the Sand Dunes at Mōkapu, O'ahu, Hawai'i," *International Surgery*, 45 (1966) 209–10.

4. See the comment by Nathaniel B. Emerson in David Malo, *Hawaiian Antiquities* [1898] (Honolulu: Bishop Museum Press, 1951), p. 183, note 34; Samuel Kamakau, *Ka Po'e Kahiko: The People of Old* (Honolulu: The Bishop Museum Press, 1964), pp. 12, 64; Handy and Pukui, *The Polynesian Family System*, p. 204; Kamakau, *Ruling Chiefs*, p. 154; and, on this and the practice of sacrifice in general, see Valerio Valeri, *Kingship and Sacrifice: Ritual and Society in Ancient Hawai'i* (Chicago: University of Chicago Press, 1985), passim, but especially chapter 4. The quoted early visitor who observed no human sacrifices during his 13 month stay is Archibald Campbell, *A Voyage Round the World*, pp. 128–29.

5. Bowers, "Pathological and Functional Changes," 209–10; Peter R. Cox, *Demography*, Fourth Edition (Cambridge: Cambridge University Press, 1970), pp. 319, 361; Donald J. Bogue, *Principles of Demography* (New York: Wiley, 1969), p. 34; Ehrlich, Ehrlich, and Holdren, *Ecoscience*, p. 199.

6. On ancient Hawaiian medical practices regarding pregnancy, see June Gutmanis, *Kāhuna Lā'au Lapa'au* (Honolulu: Island Heritage Press, 1976), pp. 31–38. For the subsequent references in this paragraph, see Samuel C. Bartlett, D.D., *Sketches of the Missions of the American Board* (Boston: ABCFM, 1872), p. 41; Kirch, *Feathered Gods and Fishhooks*, p. 287; see also Kirch's *Evolution of the Polynesian Chiefdoms*, p. 108. I have written to Professor Kirch for the source of this assertion (apart from 19th century missionary and missionary-inspired tall tales), but have received no reply. Credit for invention of this myth probably belongs to missionary William Ellis, *Journal*, pp. 327–31. I discuss this and related matters in some detail in "Recounting the Fables of Savagery: Infanticide in Ancient Hawai'i and the Functions of Political Myth," paper read at Pacific Coast Branch Meeting of the American Historical Association (1986), publication forthcoming.

7. Samwell, "Some Account of a Voyage," p. 1182. Captain Clerke also comments on the enormous number of children in his "Journal," p. 593. On infanticide in 18th and 19th century Europe see William L. Langer, "Infanticide: A Historical Survey," *History of Childhood Quarterly*, 1 (1974), 353–65; and Thomas R. Forbes, "Deadly Parents: Child Homicide in Eighteenth and Nineteenth Century England," *The Journal of the History of Medicine and Allied Sciences*, 41 (1986), 175–99. On the foundling hospitals that were in large part a response to wholesale infanticide, but which themselves wound up killing tens of thousands of children, see Ruth K. McClure, *Coram's Children: The London Foundling Hospital in the Eighteenth Century* (New Haven: Yale University Press, 1981); and Rachel Fuchs, *Abandoned Children: Foundlings and Child Welfare in Nineteenth-Century France* (Albany: State University of New York Press, 1984).

8. John Turnbull, *Voyages in the Pacific Ocean* (London, 1810), p. 229; Charles E. Snow, *Early Hawaiians*, p. 7; King, "Journal," p. 629; see also King, *The Three Voyages of Captain James Cook*, Volume VII, pp. 116–17, where he describes the

deformed people encountered, including hunchbacks, dwarfs, a man born without hands or feet, and another who had, the Hawaiians said, been born blind. For the confirming reference from an 1818 visit, see Adelbert von Chamisso, *A Voyage Around the World With the Romanzov Exploring Expedition in the Years 1815-1818* [originally published in 1821] (Honolulu: University of Hawai'i Press, 1986), p. 313.

9. Handy and Pukui, *The Polynesian Family System*, p. 79.

10. Kirch, *Feathered Gods and Fishhooks*, p. 243. Snow, *Early Hawaiians*, pp. 80-81, 9, note 8; Toni L. Han, Stephen D. Clark, Anne Garland, and Sara L. Collins, *Moe Kau Ho'oilo: Hawaiian Mortuary Practices at Keōpū, Kona, Hawai'i* (Honolulu: Bishop Museum Dept. of Anthropology Report 86-1, 1986), p. 167; Mary Kilbourne Matossian, "Death in London," *Journal of Interdisciplinary History*, 16 (1985), 188; James W. Glover, *United States Life Tables: 1890, 1901, 1910, and 1901-1910* (Washington, D.C.: Government Printing Office, 1921). I should note that another significant burial site has been studied at 'Anaeho'omalu on the island of Hawai'i. The 69 skeletons examined are presumed to date from at least as early as the 18th century and once again the age skewing is heavily toward adult individuals; only about 10 percent are subadults. However, no indication of infant mortality is provided. See Michael Pietrusewsky, *Human Skeletal Remains at 'Anaeho'omalu* (Honolulu: Bishop Museum, 1971), p. 39.

11. Douglas G. Sutton, "Maori Demographic Change, 1769-1840: The Inner Workings of 'A Picturesque But Illogical Simile,' " *Journal of the Polynesian Society*, 95 (1986), 291-339; Hassan, *Demographic Archaeology*, pp. 140-41. The required net reproductive rate to achieve my posited 0.52 percent annual growth rate is 1.11. The net reproductive rate of the cited simulation by Hassan is 1.15. Key among Sutton's "questionable osteological assumptions" is his uncritical acceptance of forensic life expectancy figures derived from techniques now known to be biased towards short life expectancy estimates (see discussion of the work of Bocquet-Appel, et al, in Chapter 2, note 20) and—most important—his use as an evidentiary centerpiece of a very small sample of exhumed female pelves in estimating the average number of births per adult pre-*pakeha* Maori woman. This sample size problem is compounded by the fact that the technique employed in making these estimates (the examination of pelvic pits and grooves acquired through pregnancy and parturition) has been shown to be exceedingly unreliable. Not only has it been found that the osteological evidence commonly becomes obliterated by old age, but repeated studies have revealed cases of heavily marked pelves in childless women, unmarked pelves in women who have given birth as many as ten times, and even possible "birth trauma" scars on *male* pelves. Among many such studies, see especially C. Adams Holt, "A Re-examination of Parturition Scars on the Human Female Pelvis" *American Journal of Physical Anthropology*, 49 (1978), 91-94; Marc A. Kelley, "Parturition and Pelvic Changes," *American Journal of Physical Anthropology*, 51 (1979), 541-46; and T. Bergfelder and B. Herrmann, "Estimating Fertility on the Basis of Birth-traumatic Changes in the Pubic Bone," *Journal of Human Evolution*, 9 (1980), 611-13.

12. Rev. J. F. H. Wohlers, "On the Conversion and Civilization of the Maoris of the South Island of New Zealand," *Transactions and Proceedings of the New*

Zealand Institute, 14 (1881), 134; Rev. Rufus Anderson, D.D., *The Hawaiian Islands: Their Progress and Condition Under Missionary Labors* (Boston: Gould & Lincoln, 1864), p. 276; Andrew Lind, *An Island Community: Ecological Succession in Hawai'i* (Chicago: University of Chicago Press, 1938), p. 93. For an example of the ease with which this notion has insinuated itself into conventional scholarly opinion, see the bland statement of it as "fact" in Peter Bellwood, *The Polynesians* (London: Thames and Hudson, 1987 [Revised Edition]), p. 98. On a more popular level, note that a report on the history of Moloka'i's Pelekunu Valley, broadcast in August, 1988 by Honolulu television station KGMB, referred to the 16th century as a time when "Hawaiians were starving"; in reply to an inquiry KGMB news anchor Bob Jones cited Hommon and Kirch as his sources (personal communication).

13. Kirch, *The Evolution of the Polynesian Chiefdoms*, pp. 107–08; Kirch, *Feathered Gods and Fishhooks*, p. 288; Patrick V. Kirch, "The Impact of the Prehistoric Polynesians on the Hawaiian Ecosystem," *Pacific Science*, 36 (1982), esp. 4–7.

14. Holmes, ed., *Captain Cook's Final Voyage*, p. 103; Clerke, "Journal," p. 573. The ratio of children to adults in a population is "a common barometer of significant dietary stress," points out B. Abbott Segraves in a summary analysis, "The Malthusian Proposition and Nutritional Stress," in Lawrence S. Greene, ed., *Malnutrition, Behavior, and Social Organization* (New York: Academic Press, 1977), p. 176; in this same volume, see also Georgeda Buchbinder's "Nutritional Stress and Postcontact Population Decline Among the Mareng of New Guinea," esp. pp. 115–121, where the same point is made graphically clear in a detailed case study.

15. See the extensive discussion on cultural responses to declining resources, including infanticide and restricted sexual activity, in Virginia Abernethy, *Population Pressure and Cultural Adjustment* (New York: Human Sciences Press, 1979), passim. Marshall Sahlins, *Islands of History* (Chicago: University of Chicago Press, 1985), p. 9. On the tendency of populations pushed to the edge of scarcity to restrain vigorous leisure activities, see Joshua Rubin, Nancy M. Flowers, and Daniel R. Gross, "The Adaptive Dimensions of Leisure," *American Ethnologist*, 13 (1986), 524–29.

16. Ellis, *An Authentic Narrative of a Voyage*, pp. 73–74; King, "Journal," p. 498. On Europe see Alfred W. Crosby, Jr., "The Early History of Syphilis: A Reappraisal," in his *The Columbian Exchange: Biological and Cultural Consequences of 1492* (Westport, Connecticut: Greenwood Press, 1972), pp. 122–64; cf. Francisco Guerra, "The Dispute Over Syphilis: Europe versus America," *Clio Medica*, 13 (1978), 39–61.

17. William Bayly, "Log," cited in Beaglehole, ed., *Journals of Captain James Cook*, Volume III, Part One, p. 233, note 4; Rickman, *Journal of Captain Cook's Last Voyage*, p. 191; Samwell, "Some Account of a Voyage," pp. 1219, 1221. On London advertisements for cures for V.D. see Lawrence Stone, *The Family, Sex, and Marriage in England, 1500–1800* (New York: Harper & Row, 1977), p. 600.

18. There is no doubt that Cook's crew spread tuberculosis: William Anderson, Cook's linguist and chief translator, who probably was in more frequent close contact with the natives than anyone from either ship, was wracked with

tuberculosis for the duration of the voyage and died of it between the time of the ships' first and second visits to Hawai'i; Captain Clerke was similarly incapacitated by the disease during the entire stay in Hawai'i and died of it a few months after the ships' final departure; and others—including King and Cook himself—either died of unspecified "lingering" illnesses while on the voyage, of tuberculosis later (King), or (in Cook's case) at least have been suspected by subsequent medical authorities of having tuberculosis while in the islands. See Sir James Watt, "Medical Aspects and Consequences of Cook's Voyages," in Robin Fisher and Hugh Johnston, eds., *Captain James Cook and His Times* (Seattle: University of Washington Press, 1979), pp. 129–57. Symptoms that probably were influenza (though they could also have been early stages of tuberculosis), and which "were pretty general" and had begun to cause death by the time the ships departed, are reported in Ellis, *An Authentic Narrative of a Voyage*, p. 151. On the possibility that what Ellis observed was tuberculosis and not influenza, note the similarity of his description ("coughs and colds . . . a violent griping or colic") with the brief discussion of occasional early symptoms of T.B. ("often so unspecific as to be dismissed under the name of cold or grippe") in René *and Jean Dubos, The White Plague: Tuberculosis, Man and Society* (Boston: Little, Brown, 1952), p. 4. Significantly, there is no evidence of any similar disease among pre-*haole* Hawaiians. On disease-specific mortality in London at this time see Matossian, "Death in London, 1750–1909," 183–97.

19. Ledyard, *Journal of Captain Cook's Last Voyage*, p. 139; Portlock, *A New, Complete, and Universal Collection*, p. 94. On tuberculosis morbidity and mortality in late 18th century England, as well as its extraordinary infectious potential, see Selman A. Waksman, *The Conquest of Tuberculosis* (Berkeley: University of California Press, 1964), pp. 19, 202.

20. On the matter of different bronchial cilia in Polynesians, see the following: J. R. Hinds, "Bronchiectasis in the Maori," *New Zealand Medical Journal*, 57 (1958), 328–32; David Waite, et al, "Cilia and Sperm Tail Abnormalities in Polynesian Bronchiectatics," *The Lancet*, no. 8081 (July 15, 1978), 132–33; and St. John Wakefield and David Waite, "Abnormal Cilia in Polynesians with Bronchiectasis," *American Review of Respiratory Disease*, 121 (1980), 1003–1010. I am grateful to University of Hawai'i science librarian Nina Horio for bringing these and related studies to my attention. On the thrifty genotype hypothesis regarding diabetes (first proposed by J. V. Neel in 1962), see the summary discussion in Paul Zimmet and Sunny Whitehouse, "Pacific Islands of Nauru, Tuvalu, and Western Samoa" in H. C. Trowell and D. P. Burkitt, eds., *Western Diseases: Their Emergence and Prevention* (London: Edward Arnold, 1981), pp. 204–24. The subsequent citations in this paragraph come from René and Jean Dubos, *The White Plague*, p. 10; Waksman, *The Conquest of Tuberculosis*, p. 175; Dubos, *Man Adapting*, p. 175; McNeill, *Plagues and Peoples*, p. 61; and Mele A. Look, *A Mortality Study of The Hawaiian People* (Honolulu: State Department of Health, 1982), pp. 4, 12.

21. Crosby, "The Early History of Syphilis," pp. 122, 151–52.

22. Ambrose King and Claude Nicol, *Venereal Diseases* (London: Bailliere Tindall & Casell, 1969), pp. 76, 78. On the effects of tuberculosis on fertility, see

Joseph A. McFalls, Jr. and Marguerite Harvey McFalls, *Disease and Fertility* (London: Academic Press, 1984), Chapter 3—with quoted passage on p. 98.

23. Samwell, "Some Account of a Voyage," p. 1178; Clerke, "Journal," p. 593; Snow, *Early Hawaiians*, pp. 53-55.

24. M. Rollin, M.D., "Dissertation on the Inhabitants of Easter Island and the Island of Mowee," in Pérouse, *A Voyage Round the World*, volume II, p. 337, emphasis added.

25. Pérouse, *A Voyage Round the World*, Volume I, pp. 347-48. The comparison of the infectious rates of syphilis and AIDS is from Michael J. Fumento, *The Myth of Heterosexual AIDS* (New York: Basic Books, forthcoming). The cited 20 to 50 percent infection rate contains an important gender differential: syphilis, like most sexually transmitted diseases, is more easily transmitted from male to female.

26. R. Ted Steinbock, *Paleopathological Diagnosis and Interpretation: Bone Diseases in Ancient Human Populations* (Springfield, Illinois: Thomas, 1976), p. 263. On the absence of rickets in pre-contact skeletons, see Bowers, "Pathological and Functional Changes," 214. On the gender differential in renal failure, see Claus Christiansen and Birgitte Hartnack, "Is Bone Loss in Chronic Renal Failure Sex Dependent?" *The Lancet* (June 25, 1977), p. 1370.

27. R. E. Hope-Simpson and D. B. Golubev, "A New Concept of the Epidemic Process of Influenza A Virus," *Epidemiology and Infection*, 99 (1987), 5-54; Dobyns, *Their Number Become Thinned*, p. 18; Dobyns, "Estimating Aboriginal American Population," p. 409; Crosby, *Ecological Imperialism*, p. 197. On the influenza epidemic that gripped England during the months that Cook was outfitting his ships and putting his crews together, see Creighton, *History of Epidemics in Britain*, Volume II, pp. 359-61.

28. Peter Pirie, "The Consequences of Cook's Hawaiian Contacts on the Local Population," in Jane N. Hurd and Michiko Kodama, eds., *Captain Cook and the Pacific Islands* (Honolulu: University of Hawai'i Pacific Islands Studies Program, 1978), p. 81.

29. Bowers, "Pathological and Functional Changes," 208; Han, Clark, Garland, and Collins, *Moe Kau a Ho'oilo*; Steinbock, *Paleopathological Diagnosis*, pp. 142, 149; Peter M. Moodie, "Yaws, Pinta, and Bejel," in Abraham I. Braude, ed., *Infectious Diseases and Medical Microbiology*, 2nd Edition (Philadelphia: W. B. Saunders, 1986), pp. 1361-66; P. W. Wilson and M. S. Mathis, "Epidemiology and Pathology of Yaws: Based on a Study of 1423 Consecutive Cases in Haiti," *Journal of the American Medical Association*, 94 (1930), 1289-92.

30. Watt, "Medical Aspects and Consequences," p. 152; King and Nicol, *Venereal Diseases*, pp. 7-8, 256; Moodie, "Yaws, Pinta, and Bejel," pp. 1361-62.

31. Lent C. Johnson and Ellis R. Kerley, "Report on Pathological Specimens from Mōkapu," in Snow, *Early Hawaiians*, p. 150. For a good, brief discussion of the frequency of skeletal involvement in tuberculosis, which shows by comparison how infinitesimal to the point of non-existence is the ambiguous evidence from Hawai'i, see Steinbock, *Paleopathological Diagnosis*, p. 175.

32. Snow, *Early Hawaiians*, p. 11; Kirch, *Feathered Gods and Fishhooks*, p. 243; Paul L. Cleghorn, Review of *Feathered Gods and Fishhooks*, *The Journal of the Polynesian Society*, 96 (1987), 133, emphasis added.

PART TWO
Critical Commentary and Reply

It is common practice in a number of scholarly journals to invite critical comments of a work in the same issue in which the work is published, followed by a reply by the author of the original work. This is particularly valuable when the work in question seeks to overturn long-settled opinion, as it permits readers immediate access to expert discussion of the main issues under debate. In this spirit, Eleanor C. Nordyke and Robert C. Schmitt—generally considered the leading demographers in the study of Hawaiʻi's population, and proponents of the belief that the pre-1778 population was between 200,000 and 300,000—were invited, without restrictions, to provide critical commentary on David Stannard's analysis and new population estimate. Their comments and Stannard's reply are contained in the pages that follow.

COMMENT
By Eleanor C. Nordyke
Research Fellow
East-West Population Institute
East-West Center

David Stannard's extensively researched and well written monograph reawakens the question of what number of people resided in Hawai'i before the arrival of foreign persons to the Islands in the last quarter of the eighteenth century. I appreciate the opportunity to respond, as requested, "to the controversial argument of the paper—and the necessarily speculative nature of all precensal estimates." Although Stannard's population conclusions seem beyond statistical, demographic, or historical probability, the paper offers an intriguing and different approach to the question of numbers of inhabitants in ancient Hawai'i.

The final answer to this question may be derived from an archaeological study on Moloka'i in 1909 by John Stokes, former Curator of Polynesian Ethnology at B. P. Bishop Museum, if the reference to "heiau" is paraphrased to "population":

> One thing forcibly brought home to the writer on this island as on the island of Hawai'i was the futility of seeking ancient information today concerning heiau [numbers of population]. The heiau are there and the natives can show them, but the information died with the grandfathers of the present old men.[1]

Here are a few of my thoughts regarding Stannard's paper, which henceforth will be referred to as "Stannard".

1. Stannard suggests acceptance of a pre-1778 population figure that far exceeds all estimated numbers that have been made in the past two centuries by Pacific voyagers and by historic and demographic scholars. Although this proposed theory offers an interesting intellectual exercise, these new population numbers remain inconclusive and speculative in the absence of deliberate anthro-

pologic and archaeologic investigation and without an authentic census or sample survey.

2. Stannard often questions or denigrates the population figures given by Robert C. Schmitt in his "New Estimates of the Pre-Censal Population of Hawai'i".[2] Schmitt, Hawai'i State Statistician, has pursued meticulous research on Hawaiian subjects for over 40 years. He has worked in conjunction with other Hawai'i population authorities, such as Romanzo Adams, Andrew Lind, and Bernhard Hormann, when presenting pre-censal population figures, and he has published an array of books and articles with thorough documentation. His carefully prepared contributions are rooted in cautious statements that recognize limitations when using assumptions in the absence of facts. Schmitt's writings clearly delineate the softness of the data for ancient Hawai'i and its hypothetical content, but his breadth of knowledge and his alliance with other population scholars offer credence to an acceptance of pre-1778 population figures closer to his suggested findings than to the high numbers proposed in this study.

3. The term "pre-*haole*", used in reference to the period prior to the arrival of foreigners in 1778, seems inappropriate. In recent years in Hawai'i, the word *haole* has been associated with a white person, although formerly it represented anything foreign or introduced, including plants and animals. It has been interpreted as meaning *ha* (breath) *'ole* (without), in reference to persons who could not speak the Hawaiian language.

The use of the term "pre-*haole*" presents a negative racial overtone that detracts from this study. Samuel M. Kamakau, Hawaiian historian, wrote: "Many foreigners of different races, the red, the black, the white, came in early days to Hawaii."[3] The traditional reference of "pre-contact", pre-1778, pre-historic, or "ancient Hawai'i" would identify this early era with greater precision.

4. The population totals presented by Stannard, unadjusted and adjusted, seem to be inflated beyond reasonable estimate (Table 1). For example, for the island of Ni'ihau Captain James King, in completing Cook's voyage description in 1789, assigned 14,000 persons to that small area; Stannard's count ranged from a high of 7,774 to a low of 3,650 persons, Schmitt and others suggested 500 to 1,000 inhabitants. Captain Cook wrote in 1778:

> ... The ground, through which I passed, was in a state of nature, very stony, and the soil seemed poor. ... Our people, who had been obliged to remain so long on shore, gave me the same account of those parts of the island which they had traversed. They met with several salt ponds, some of which had a little water remaining, but others had none; and the salt that was left in them was so thin, that no great quantity could have been procured. There was no appearance of any running stream; and though they found some small wells, in which the fresh water was tolerably good, it seems scarce. The habitations of the natives were thinly scattered about, and, it was supposed, that there *could not be more than five hundred people upon the island* [underlined for emphasis] as the greatest part were seen at the marketing-place of our party, and few found about the houses by those who walked up the country.[4]

In contrast to Stannard's assumption of increased density of inland population, King wrote:

> It may be thought extremely difficult to form any probable conjectures respecting the population of islands, with many parts of which we are but imperfectly acquainted. There are, however, two circumstances, that take away much of this objection; the first is, that the interior parts of the country are entirely uninhabited; so that, if the number of the inhabitants along the coast be known, the whole will be pretty accurately determined. The other is, that there are no towns of any considerable size, the habitations of the natives being pretty equally dispersed in small villages round all their coasts.[5]

Abraham Fornander, a nineteenth century compiler of ancient Polynesian history from native legends and reports, opposes King's estimate of 54,000 inhabitants for Kaua'i in 1779 and Stannard's population figure of about 82,000 residents by suggesting 24,000 to 52,000 fewer inhabitants:

> It is probable that Cook's estimate of the populousness of Kaua'i is too high. Judging from the section of the island that he saw, and taking the village of Waimea as a standard, he estimated sixty such villages on the island, with a total of 30,000 inhabitants. The ancient native division of the island gives no account of so many villages as Cook [or Stannard] supposed . . .[6]

5. There is some question about Stannard's hypothesis that "in every case the lush windward sides of the islands were settled first, with expansion into the drier areas generally occurring only when

Table 1. Population Estimates by Island, Hawai'i, 1778

	Total	Hawai'i	Maui[a]	Lāna'i	Moloka'i	O'ahu	Kaua'i	Ni'ihau
King	400,000	150,000	65,400	20,400	36,000	60,200	54,000	14,000
Bligh	242,000	100,000	40,000	1,000	20,000	40,000	40,000	1,200
Emory	300,000	120,000	75,000	3,500	10,000	60,000	30,000	1,500
Others[b]	—	100,000	—	—	—	—	30,000	500
Schmitt								
High	250,000	100,000	60,000	4,000	10,000	50,000	30,000	1,000
Low	200,000	80,000	45,000	3,000	8,000	35,000	20,000	500
Stannard								
Unadjusted	967,556	340,000	260,925	11,879	44,549	220,927	81,502	7,774
Adjusted	795,343	403,800	125,021	13,950	44,387	121,540	82,995	3,650
Nordyke[c]	310,000	120,000	70,000	4,000	15,000	60,000	40,000	1,000

SOURCE: Schmitt, Robert C. "New Estimates of the Pre-Censal Population of Hawai'i," *The Journal of the Polynesian Society*, 1971, Vol. 80, No. 2, pp. 241-242.

[a]Includes Kaho'olawe, between 50 and 100 in Schmitt's figure, and 594 in Stannard's first assumption and 1,125 in his adjustment.
[b]Hawai'i population estimate by John Ledyard; Kaua'i and Ni'ihau figures by James Cook.
[c]Present estimate

the densities of the windward areas were sufficient to require such expansion. The repeated evidence of substantial pre-*haole* Hawaiian settlements in the harshest environments *means that the more hospitable environments must long before have been filled to capacity* [underlined for emphasis]."

While some settlement occurred on the windward side of the island chain, much of the population observed by early voyagers was located on the leeward side of the islands. There is no archaeological evidence to substantiate a claim that the windward areas were "filled to capacity" before habitation occurred on the southern, drier areas. Probably the people settled where the land was receptive to cultivation, where fresh water and shade was available, and where fishing was accessible. In a report on the distribution of Moloka'i's population in 1853, John W. Coulter reported:

> ... The outstanding characteristic of the distribution and density of people was the concentration along the eastern third of the south coast. ... The rainfall of the southeastern part of the island afforded sufficient water in the stream valleys for their lower flood plains to be used for wet land agriculture. ... Fish were easily procurable on most of the eastern half of the south coast.[7]

The question remains: where did the ancient Hawaiians live? The *ahupua'a* land divisions extended from the uplands to the sea. Hawai'i anthropologists indicate the *maka'āinana*, or commoners, resided primarily along the coast of the ahupua'a, using the uplands for agricultural projects. Archaeologists do not believe that the natives lived inland in large numbers, nor did they reside densely in wet windward areas. Most of the people probably occupied small villages scattered unevenly along habitable coastline. It is interesting to observe that most of the major sites of ali'i residences occurred on the leeward side of each island—at Kailua-Kona on Hawai'i, at Lahaina on Maui, in the Kona district of Moloka'i, at Honolulu on O'ahu, and at Waimea on Kaua'i.

6. The initial date of habitation, the annual rate of growth, and the resulting total population number in prehistoric Hawai'i as assumed by Stannard are probably overstated. The comment ". . . it is now known that the first human settlers arrived in Hawai'i at least as early as the first century A.D." (p. 32) may be questioned. Using charcoal, wood, bones, sea urchins spines, and

other organic material, scientists have assessed the radiocarbon age of many localities and provided a fairly solid framework for early chronological history. According to archaeologist Patrick Kirch:

> ... It is probable that the first settlement of Hawai'i occurred sometime *before* the fourth to fifth century. At present, it is difficult on strictly archaeological grounds to be more precise as to the date of initial colonization of the Hawaiian Islands. In my own view, given that a number of permanent settlements were distributed throughout all of the main islands by the sixth century, it is likely that the first colonization occurred some two or three centuries earlier, perhaps by A.D. 300. . . . Until more early sites are found and excavated, however, this is nothing more than the considered opinion of one archaeologist—and I should note that not all of my colleagues agree.[8]

The geometric progression of an assumed population at an unvarying annual growth rate has demographic limitations. Biometricians have described a logistic, or S-curve, of population growth that refutes the concept of unrestrained multiplication of humankind. In the twentieth century in Hawai'i, the steady growth of population has been the result of high fertility in the early decades, continued rapid in-migration and controlled mortality; this rate of change would not be expected to continue as rates of fertility and migration decrease.

In contrast, ancient Hawai'i responded to migration and mortality influences. The small population of early ocean seafarers, probably constrained initially by a low proportion of women, increased gradually in the absence of fertility control. However, the introduction of diseases from occasional migrants and the imposition of warring strangers altered the pattern of steady population growth.

In a family history by Pali Lee and Koko Willis, ancient Hawai'i is described from the oral history of a woman who lived on Moloka'i from 1816 to 1931 and who had been entrusted by her elders to retain the knowledge of the ancient days and to teach new generations about Hawaiian culture and religion. While the authors say that historians and anthropologists may differ with some of their material, they present a unique view of old Hawai'i.

... Seven or eight hundred years ago the Tahitians came to our islands, and since then the stories of our origins and life have been dominated by their outlook. In many ways the Tahitians were a people similar to us, but in many others we are as light is to the dark.

... Pa'ao had gone back to Tahiti and gathered thousands of people to come to Hawai'i and take over the land. The men were tall fierce warriors. They did not believe in the force of light, only in the force of the closed fist, in mighty armies that killed, took and plundered.—Soon the sea did turn red with the blood of our people as thousands were slaughtered and enslaved.—[9]

Mortality in prehistoric Hawai'i may be attributed to wars, homicide, accidents, abortion and infanticide, prevalent diseases such as pneumonia and gastrointestinal disorders, unstable nutrition related to incidences of famine and drought, and lack of modern sanitation. According to Hawaiian historian Samuel Kamakau:

The constant wars of old days were another cause of depopulation. Among the noncombatants even women were cut down, and little children killed. In Puna, Hawai'i at Opihikao, a battle was fought in which even pregnant women and children were slain. . . . Those were indeed bloody days . . .

Infanticide was another evil practiced in pagan days and still made use of today. Women dispose of their children in secret places with the help of their husbands, parents, and of the *kahuna 'o'o*, and others besides. Women in old days killed the child within the womb by drinking medicine to poison the child, by using a sharp-pointed instrument, by beating on the abdomen, or they would throw a newborn infant in to the water or bury it in the earth. Their reasons for killing the child were age, poverty, pleasure-seeking, illicit relations, jealousy, slavery, dislike of children, and shame.[10]

7. The rate of decline of Hawaiian population suggested by Stannard, seen in the steep drop of the line in the graph shown in Figure 5 (p. 51), is overstated because the population probably never achieved the initial high figures that he proposes. Much of the mortality that took place after 1778 occured some years after the first exploring expeditions. This population loss was monitored in journals of voyagers and by missionary writings. The rate of depopulation for 1778–1888 is probably more accurately graphed by Schmitt's trajectory A of Figure 4 (p. 51). While

Cook's men introduced venereal diseases that affected fertility outcome, the rate of population decline was probably higher in response to specific infections—cholera, measles, whooping cough, smallpox, leprosy, tuberculosis—from people who arrived in increasing numbers on ships in the nineteenth century.

Moloka'i's 1778 population, estimated at about 44,500 persons by Stannard, at 36,000 persons by Captain King, and at 10,500 inhabitants by Archaeologist Kenneth Emory, is assumed to have suffered less population decline than other islands. According to Anthropologist Catherine Summers:

> The small decrease in Moloka'i's population [from Emory's estimate of 10,500 for 1779 to the *Missionary Herald* report of 8,700 in 1836], as compared with that of the four major islands, can be accounted for by the fact that Moloka'i being one of the lesser islands and affording but poor anchorage, was not frequently visited by white men. Consequently, the populace was not exposed to the diseases that killed off so many of the natives on the larger islands. The decrease in population was probably due to the natives' leaving Moloka'i for one of the larger islands.[11]

8. Stannard's suggested pre-1778 population total of 795,000–967,000 seems unreasonable when considered in terms of basic needs of the population.

What was the food supply for nearly a million people? In 1970, when Hawai'i's population was counted at 769,913 inhabitants, 80 percent of the food supply was imported. Could ancient Hawai'i, using primitive farming and fishing methods, have provided for such a dense population? Where is the evidence of such intense agricultural activity? How was food stored and preserved?

What was the water supply? Were there any reservoirs or water distribution systems to accomodate so many people?

If there had been such an acute loss of life in the first fifty years of post-contact Hawai'i, wouldn't the earliest voyagers (Portlock and Dixon, Vancouver, Delano, Kotzebue, and others) have written in great detail about it, and wouldn't burial sites indicate this loss if the numbers had dropped from Stannard's near-million in 1779 to just 130,000 counted residents in 1831?

As much as I would like to agree with Stannard's assumptions, I find that it is not possible to accept the high figures he proposes for Hawai'i's pre-1778 population. Until an anthropologic or archaeological assessment verifies increased population density in the highlands of the islands or until other conclusive scientific data is presented, I must reject the suggested figures given in this paper and endorse the previous findings of Hawai'i's authorities of history and demography.

NOTES

1. John F. G. Stokes, "Heiau," undated manuscript in Library of the Bishop Museum.

2. *The Journal of the Polynesian Society*, 80 (1971), 237–43.

3. Samuel M. Kamakau, *Ruling Chiefs of Hawai'i* (Honolulu: Kamehameha Schools Press, 1961), p. 245.

4. Captain James Cook, *A Voyage to the Pacific Ocean Undertaken, by the Command of His Majesty, for Making Discoveries in the Northern Hemisphere* (London: G. Nicol and T. Cadell, 1784), Volume 2, p. 218.

5. Ibid., pp. 127–28.

6. Abraham Fornander, *An Account of the Polynesian Race, Its Origins and Migrations* (London: Trubner & Co., 1880), Vol. II, p. 165.

7. John Wesley Coulter, *Population and Utilization of Land and Sea in Hawai'i, 1853* (Bernice P. Bishop Museum Bulletin 88, 1931), p. 20.

8. Patrick V. Kirch, *Feathered Gods and Fishhooks: An Introduction to Hawaiian Archaeology and Prehistory* (Honolulu: University of Hawai'i Press, 1985), pp. 68–69.

9. Pali Jae Lee and Koko Willis, *Tales From the Night Rainbow* (Honolulu: Paia-Kapela-Willis Ohana, 1987) pp. xi, 17, and 23–25.

10. Kamakau, *Ruling Chiefs*, pp. 233–34.

11. Catherine C. Summers, "Moloka'i: A Site Survey," *Pacific Anthropological Records, Number 14* (Honolulu: Bishop Museum Press, 1971), p. 3.

COMMENT

By Robert C. Schmitt
State Statistician
Hawai'i State Department of Business
and Ecomonic Development

All persons interested in Hawai'i's demographic history should be grateful to David E. Stannard for his impressive monograph, *Before the Horror: The Population of Hawai'i on the Eve of Western Contact*. For almost two centuries, the question of Hawai'i's pre-contact population has engendered controversy and produced a wide range of retrospective estimates. Most earlier analysts, unfortunately, limited their discussions to brief summary statements providing only the barest basis for subsequent evaluation. Professor Stannard, in contrast, offers a far-ranging, comprehensive and heavily documented review of all the evidence, including recent archaeological findings not available to earlier commentators. Even among those who are unable to reach the same conclusions, such scholarship demands respect.

At the heart of Stannard's analysis is a proposed upward revision in past estimates of Hawai'i's population in 1778, vastly higher than those of his predecessors. Earlier estimates have ranged from less than 100,000 to a high of 500,000. Most have fallen between 200,000 and 400,000, and the consensus, if such existed, seemed to favor a figure in the 250,000–300,000 range. Now, in a radical break with past writers, Stannard proposes a pre-contact total at least as high as 800,000, which he regards as "a restrained and modest figure."

In attacking earlier estimates, Stannard focuses on my 1971 research note, "New Estimates of the Pre-Censal Population of Hawai'i."[1] In that short article, I suggested a 1778 total "not over 250,000, and possibly as low as 200,000." The major aim of the article, however, was to provide pre-1832 estimates for individual islands more consistent with 1831–1832 census results than were available from contemporary estimates. A secondary goal was to re-evaluate the factors in the massive depopulaton that had occurred, stressing "low fertility (a result of venereal disease, abortion, and other factors), heavy infant mortality, normally high adult death rates, and out-migration," rather than the traditionally cited effects of famines, wars, epidemics, infanticide, and human sacrifice.

My reasons for recommending a relatively low set of estimates were summarized in the following passage:

> Demographers have observed, for example, that "the depletion of primitive peoples have probably been exaggerated in many cases," by the natives themselves as well as by navigators, missionaires, and administrators. Guesses of the size of crowds—a frequent element in these pre-censal estimates—are notoriously unreliable, typically producing totals two or three times the actual number. The deserted villages and fields which early visitors and settlers interpreted as evidence of massive depopulation were in reality the result of internal migration; Shaler, writing in 1805, noted that Kamehameha's frequent changes in residence forced similar shifts on his chiefs and consequently their people—"Everything is abandoned to follow the sovereign, and the country being deserted by all who have an interest in its cultivation and improvement of the lands, they are of course neglected." Great disasters like the 1804 epidemic, the wars of the late eighteenth century, and the famines of 1796, 1806-7, 1812 and 1824-5 appear to have caused far fewer deaths than hitherto believed.

It should be emphasized that estimates of 300,000 or less have been accepted by a number of modern authorities, all of them far more eminent than the present author, and several still living. The most thorough study of Hawaiian population trends appears to be that made by the late Romanzo Adams, for many years professor of sociology at the University of Hawai'i. After careful consideration, Adams (whose analysis remains in manuscript) settled on a pre-contact total of 300,000. This figure was also accepted by Adams' younger colleagues, Andrew W. Lind and Bernhard L. Hormann, as well as by Kenneth P. Emory.[2] More recently, Kirch has outlined a pre-contact growth curve rising from 100 at first settlement (dated by him between A.D. 300 and 600) to 1,000 in A.D. 600, 20,000 in 1100, 200,000 in 1650, and 250,000 in 1778.[3] Sir Peter Buck was quoted in 1951 as estimating the total on contact as "perhaps 100,000 or more, but not above 150,000."[4] Stannard (citing Daws) reports that Norma McArthur shortly before her death "was heading toward the extraordinary conclusion that the pre-*haole* population of Hawai'i was less than 100,000."

Although the foregoing list hardly constitutes a convincing refutation of Stannard's main points, it does demonstrate a widespread conviction among past analysts—many of whom were obviously well qualified to offer an opinion—that the 1778 total was lower, and not higher, than the estimate of 400,000 published by King.

One of the more striking aspects of Stannard's analysis is his advocacy of a 1778 total actually greater than that found in the Islands in any peacetime year before the 1970s. The population of Hawai'i declined from its 1778 total (whatever it was) to an all-time low of 53,900 in 1876, and then began a long, virtually uninterrupted rise to its present level. It did not reach 300,000 (again?) until 1924, and 400,000 until 1937. During World War II, when more than 400,000 U.S. troops were temporarily stationed in the Territory, the population briefly soared to 859,000, but the return of peace brought about a resumption of the long-term trend. The population finally passed 800,000 in 1971 and 1,000,000 in 1983, and in 1986, the most recent date available at this writing, stood at 1,062,000.[5] The possibility that modern Hawai'i, after more than a century of declining death rates, prolonged high levels of net in-migration, and the absorption of countless acres for urban and suburban housing (much of it high-rise), can support a population not much greater than that present before 1778, when economic resources and available technology were vastly more limited, may seem highly unlikely to many observers.

Much of Professor Stannard's defense of his revolutionary estimate is based on comparative data for other areas at the time of their initial contacts with Europeans. Both insular populations, primarily those in the Caribbean and Pacific, and continental peoples, chiefly in North and South America, are included in his analysis.

In part, he reasons that pre-contact population densities in many of these areas were supposedly far greater than those implicit in the traditionally accepted estimates for Hawai'i (about 47 per square mile, assuming 300,000 inhabitants), and therefore were seriously understated in the latter case.

Gross densities, however, can be seriously misleading. Much

depends on soil conditions, topography, and climate. A relatively flat, fertile and well-watered area (the U.S. Midwest, for example) can typically support a much larger population than a mountainous, arid, and infertile area (like the Rockies) is capable of maintaining. Although the Hawaiian Archipelago is hardly an arid desert, and certainly has access to vital ocean resources, it nonetheless suffers certain limitations. Except for the Big Island, the topography is exceptionally rugged, with 50.5 percent of the surface of Kaua'i, 45.5 percent of O'ahu, and 36.0 percent of Maui having a slope in excess of 20 percent. Rainfall ranges from too dry to too wet: the average annual precipitation is less than 15 inches in the coastal sections of South Kohala, Maui from Kaupō to Kahana, the western two-thirds of Moloka'i, and much of Kaho'olawe, Lāna'i, and Ni'ihau, yet it exceeds 150 inches in Hilo, Hāmākua, and part of O'ahu and Kaua'i. Much of the soil, moreover, is inhospitable to cultivation: a recent State study of soil productivity and the suitability of land for agriculture assigned ratings below 50 (on a scale of 100) to 86.4 percent of the surface of the Big Island and 79.6 percent of the combined area of the six largest islands.[6]

Stannard further supports his estimate by postulating a characteristic rate of decline for isolated societies following their first contacts with Westerners. This curve, he contends, plummets downward at an extremely rapid rate in the first few years, then slowly levels off before bottoming out at approximately 5 percent of the area's original population. He notes that such a ratio, applied to Hawaiian census data for 1878 or the 1890's, would indicate a far higher pre-contact population than that estimated by the present author and his predecessors. He notes, moreover, that the previously assumed total on contact in combination with existing census data indicates a more rapid decline in the second half-century than in the first 50 years after Cook's arrival, an aberration which he regards as most unlikely.

In these contentions, however, he may be overgeneralizing. Although many isolated societies have indeed suffered catastrophic declines upon their initial exposure to European diseases, others have recorded less devastating consequences. Notable examples of much more modest declines include such sister Pacific island groups of Sāmoa and Tonga.[7] The apparent acceleration of the rate of decline in Hawai'i toward the middle of the 19th century rather than in an earlier period may simply reflect Hawai'i's unique transportation history. Before the California gold rush, most shipping destined for Hawai'i sailed from the U.S. East Coast; on the long voyages thus required, many potentially contagious crewmen or passengers had ample time either to recover or die. After 1848, however, the shorter voyage from San Francisco was a much more common event, and introduced diseases became both frequent and virulent. It was not mere coincidence that Hawai'i underwent a rapid succession of major epidemics between 1848 and 1853, followed by lesser but still grievous encounters throughout the remainder of the decade.[8]

With respect to both pre-contact density and post-contact decline, Stannard relies on available estimates of the population at the time of European contact for these comparative areas. I am unable to comment on his data for North and South America and for the Caribbean, but I would urge utmost caution in accepting such estimates for most (and perhaps all) Pacific areas. Any review of early estimates for Pacific islands will invariably reveal widely divergent figures, unbridgeable gaps, obvious inconsistencies, and statistical chaos.[9]

Such problems are not limited to 17th and 18th century guesses by untrained observers for newly discovered territories. They occur even today in modern American communities, where full censuses are conducted at 10-year intervals, birth and death registration are virtually complete, and symptomatic series such as utility connections or voter registration generally reflect the direction and magnitude of migration flows. While the estimating errors made by present-day demographers with regard to U.S. communities are by no means as serious as those for an earlier period, they often go badly astray. In 1980, for example, the official estimate of the population of Hawai'i fell 36,434 short of the census count, and net growth for the decade was underestimated by 18.7 percent.[10]

In some respects, precensal population estimates have more in common with population projections and forecasts than with postcensal estimates. Forecasts, of course, are notoriously difficult to make with acceptable accuracy, as any survey of earlier projections for Hawai'i will amply attest.[11] The problems are equally formidable in constructing a retrocast, in which the population at some date long before the first firm data point is approximated. For Hawai'i, this means making a reverse extrapolation 54 years into the past. In any such effort, sizable errors would be almost inevitable.

Another issue worthy of comment is the health of the ancient Hawaiians. Stannard cites Bushnell's conclusions that "the aboriginal Hawaiians were an extraordinarily healthy people, who were afflicted with no important infectious diseases," and adds that "it is now almost certain that Hawaiians in 1778 had life expectancies greater than their European contemporaries." He also feels that the small numbers of children's remains at two major burial sites attest to a remarkably low infant mortality rate.

Not everyone would agree with this rosy assessment. David Malo, for example, recalled two exceptionally destructive epidemics, the *mai ahulau* in Waia's reign and *hai-lepo* at a later date.[12] The relative lack of infant skeletons at burial sites is hardly proof of high survival rates; it may simply reflect age differentials in the disposal of bodies. Even taking this possible underrepresentation of infants at face value, Gardner concluded from the Mōkapu age distribution that these people could not have had an expectation at birth higher than 30 years.[13] Such evidence as exists would seem to support Irene Taeuber's conclusion: "If the fertility of the pre-contact period was high, the precarious ecological balances can have been preserved only by a level of mortality that was also high."[14]

One of the more disquieting aspects of Stannard's analysis is its occasional appeals to trendiness and the scholarly bandwagon. He feels that "the American revolution in historical demography that began with Woodrow Borah and Sherburne Cook as much as fifty years ago . . . has had virtually no effect on Pacific island scholarship to date. In fact, Pacific island historical demography remains largely in an arrested state similar to that of such scholarship in the Americas of several decades ago." As noted before, however, conditions in these areas were often highly dissimilar. Each regions's estimates must be judged on their own merits, without regard to scholarly fashions.

There can be no doubt that the Hawaiian Islands suffered a catastrophic depopulation during the century following Cook's arrival. Putting exact—or even approximate—numbers on this loss is however another matter. It is hard enough to estimate the population of a modern community with acceptable accuracy. Estimating the 1778 population of a 6,425-square mile archipelago from a rough stab at the number of persons inhabiting a short stretch of beach, without the benefit of either a full-scale, all-island enumeration or modern sampling techniques, is far more difficult. The true number is ultimately unknowable.

Professor Stannard deserves considerable praise for his originality, industry, and iconoclasm. His subject is far from trivial, and his argument is provocative. But I must still vote *kānalua*.

NOTES

1. *The Journal of the Polynesian Society,* 80 (1971), pp. 237–243. Stannard also cites an unpublished paper by Robert C. Schmitt and Lynn Y. S. Zane, *How Many People Have Ever Lived in Hawai'i?* (1977), but apparently reads more into that exercise than the authors intended. That paper reported hypothetical estimates of the cumulative population of Hawai'i (that is, births plus in-migrants), based on alternative assumptions regarding date of first settlement (either A.D. 1 or A.D. 500), size of initial settlement (either 20, 100 or 500), shape of growth curve (constant rate to A.D. 1200 followed by zero growth to 1778, or constant rate throughout the pre-contact period), and number present in 1778 (200,000, 300,000, or 400,000). Six different combinations of these values were plotted, producing annual growth rates ranging from 0.45 to 0.76 percent and cumulative pre-1778 populations between 1,517,000 and 9,104,000. The authors intended these calculations merely as illustrative examples of the wide range of end-totals (that is, cumulative populations) implicit in any combination of variant assumptions, and not as a serious statement regarding the actual trend of population in pre-Cook Hawai'i.

2. These estimates are discussed more fully in my earlier work, *Demographic Statistics of Hawai'i: 1778–1965* (Honolulu: University of Hawai'i Press, 1968), Chap II.

3. Patrick Vinton Kirch, *Feathered Gods and Fishhooks* (Honolulu: University of Hawai'i Press, 1985), pp. 286, 298, 302, and 304.

4. Cited in Schmitt, *Demographic Statistics,* p. 21.

5. For annual estimates, 1832–1986, see Robert C. Schmitt, *Historical Statistics of Hawai'i* (Honolulu: University Press of Hawai'i, 1977), pp. 9–10, and Hawai'i State Department of Planning and Economic Development, *The State of Hawai'i Data Book 1986: A Statistical Abstract* (December 1986), p. 12.

6. DPED, *Data Book 1986,* p. 166, 180–181, and 525.

7. Norma McArthur, *Island Populations of the Pacific* (Canberra: Australian National University Press, and Honolulu: University of Hawai'i Press, 1968), Chapters 2 and 3.

8. Robert C. Schmitt, "The Ōku'u—Hawai'i's Greatest Epidemic," *Hawai'i Medical Journal*, 29 (May–June 1970), pp. 359–364, at p. 363.

9. See, for example, Robert C. Schmitt, "Garbled Population Estimates of Central Polynesia," in William Petersen, ed., *Readings in Population* (New York: The Macmillan Co., 1972), pp. 71–76.

10. U.S. Bureau of the Census, "Evaluation of Population Estimation Procedures for States, 1980: An Interim Report", *Current Population Reports, Population Estimates and Projections*, Series P-25, No. 933 (June 1983), p. 12.

11. See, for example, the studies described in the Hawai'i State Department of Planning and Economic Development, *Bibliography of Population Forecasts and Projections for Hawai'i, 1987* (Statistical Report 199, May 15, 1987).

12. Cited in Schmitt, "The Ōku'u," pp. 360–361.

13. Robert W. Gardner and Robert C. Schmitt, "Ninety-Seven Years of Mortality in Hawai'i," *Hawai'i Medical Journal*, 37 (October 1978), pp. 297–302.

14. Irene B. Taeuber, "Hawai'i," *Population Index*, 28 (April 1962), p. 100.

REPLY

by David E. Stannard

> Oh, happy posterity, who will not experience such abysmal woe and will look upon our testimony as a fable.
> —Petrarch, on the Black Death

Eleanor Nordyke and Robert Schmitt currently are by far the most recognized experts in matters pertaining to Hawai'i's population, past and present. Thus, it is with much appreciation and respect that I receive their comments on my work. In arranging my reply, I have chosen to combine Nordyke's and Schmitt's comments when they duplicate one another and to order them sequentially to parallel the argument of my essay. This should simplify matters and make things easiest on the reader. I shall begin, therefore, with the first area of discussion, my treatment of previous estimates from King to Schmitt.[1]

A) Nordyke says that my "new population numbers remain inconclusive and speculative in the absence of deliberate anthropologic and archaeologic investigation and without an authentic census or sample survey." I agree: as with all pre-censal estimates, including those advanced by Nordyke, Schmitt, and other previous writers, my numbers are tentative and they must remain exploratory; in fact, I said as much several times in presenting my argument. However, we are never going to have "an authentic census or sample survey" of the pre-*haole* population and my estimate relies on far more anthropological, archaeological, and other scholarly data than does any previous estimate—as Schmitt, for example, acknowledges. Indeed, virtually all previous estimates—including the estimate Nordyke accepts—refer to *no* such data whatsoever. How, then, can she conclude that such estimates, which meet none of the criteria she selectively imposes on my much more thorough estimate, are more reliable than mine? The answer to this seeming contradiction is simple: joining a somewhat more reticent Schmitt on this point, she merely asserts that earlier estimates are more credible because they were made by what she regards as "authorities." Apparently it is not, then, the content of an argument or the quality of the data that matter, but (to use Schmitt's word) the "eminent" stature of the person making the estimate—even if, as Schmitt acknowledges, such eminent persons "unfortunately, limited their discussions to brief summary statements providing only the barest basis for subsequent evaluation." (This is putting it mildly: one of Schmitt's "authoritative" citations by an eminent person turns out to be a brief and undocumented 1951 *Honolulu Star-Bulletin* editorial commentary by Peter Buck.) This, it must be said, is not the way of scholarship. If it were, we would still believe in witches, hobgoblins, and specters; after all, Sir Isaac Newton believed in them—and who was more eminent than he? The simple fact of the matter is that historical scholarship is always tentative, always in a state of change; but the credibility of an analysis, however tentative, must be based solely on the data and the undergirding logic—not on the protection of tradition or the reputations of earlier writers who were mentors or friends of the defenders in question.

B) Nordyke says that my population totals "seem to be inflated beyond reasonable estimate"—and here she does provide what she regards as evidentiary citations: Captain Cook's lower estimate of the population of Ni'ihau in 1778; Lieutenant King's belief that there was no inland population anywhere in the islands; and a statement regarding Kaua'i by Judge Abraham Fornander. It is difficult to know what to say about the first two examples, since Nordyke's comments completely ignore the fact that I dealt with these matters at some length in the text on which she is commenting. (See pp. 8–10, 25–27.) As I point out there, with supporting evidence, Cook and King were wrong: Ni'ihau's 1778 population clearly was much higher than 500 and there *were* inland settlements. As well as the citations in the text on this latter point—on inland populations from Ka'ū on Hawai'i to Hālawa, Anahulu, and Luluku on O'ahu—evidence of ancient inland habitation continues to emerge with virtually every passing year; indeed, in addition to the well known interior settlements in windward valleys on all the major islands, in just the last two years there has been reported radiocarbon and burn layer evidence of 500 year old settlements in leeward areas such as inland Kona and Waimea on Hawai'i. Moreover, it has long been known that in some locales—for instance, Mākaha on O'ahu—the inland settlements were even larger than the coastal settlements in the same *ahupua'a*.[2]

In any case, there is a difference of just 3000 people between Cook's Ni'ihau estimate and mine, and I posit a likely inland population of only 10 percent of the all-island total; as I state in the text (p. 30), even if I were wrong on both these counts (although the data are as solid as currently possible in support of my contentions) there would be minimal to no impact on my overall archipelagic estimate. Thus, there are no grounds at all for using these minor examples to conclude, as Nordyke does, that my total all-island figure is "inflated beyond reasonable estimate." As for Judge Fornander, his comment on the population of Kaua'i was both undocumented and was made in 1879—a full century of devastation after Western contact. It is no more credible a piece of historical evidence regarding pre-1778 Hawai'i than is his other comment —tellingly uncited by Nordyke because it doesn't fit her argument, though it appears in the very same quoted paragraph—that Cook's estimate of the population of Ni'ihau is plainly "underrated."

C) In the same way that Nordyke raises criticisms without mentioning that I dealt with the exact same matters in the body of my essay, Schmitt quotes his own past assertions that "demographers have observed . . . that 'the depletion of primitive peoples have probably been exaggerated in many cases' by the natives themselves as well as by navigators, missionaries, and administrators" and that "guesses of the size of crowds—a frequent element in these pre-censal estimates—are notoriously unreliable, typically producing two or three times the actual number." As I pointed out in the text (p. 5), on the first of these points Schmitt cites for support the undocumented generalization of *one* demographer (who is not a specialist in historical demography) against an overwhelming body of *historical* demographers—indeed, the most "eminent" historical demographers—whose first-hand research has led them to precisely the opposite conclusion. And what is the source of Schmitt's second confident assertion regarding the "notorious" overestimates of crowds that are "a frequent element in these pre-censal estimates"? A 1967 article in *Time* magazine on disagreements about the size of student demonstrations in Berkeley, California! If this were an isolated case it might be worth overlooking, but in fact it is only one of a number of instances in which examination of the actual source underpinning a confident assertion by Nordyke or Schmitt reveals, shall we say, a good deal less than meets the eye. Other examples—including the blatant use of patently fabricated tales and legends as historical "evidence"—are discussed in subsequent pages.

D) The final critique of this portion of the text is Nordyke's questioning of my demonstration that the windward areas of the islands were more densely populated than the leeward areas. Her central evidence in opposition here is her statement that "much of the population observed by early voyagers was located on the leeward sides of the islands" and a quotation from a report on the principal area of population concentration on Moloka'i in 1853. As to the first of these (again, discussed by me at some length, pp. 17–23), *of course* the early Western voyagers "observed" much of the Hawaiian population on the leeward sides of the islands; that is because, for the good and necessary navigational reasons that I described, they had to concentrate their close-to-shore sailing and infrequent landings on the leeward sides. This was precisely my point regarding King's *mistaken* assumption that there was an equal windward/leeward population distribution, a mistake, as I noted, corrected by the later comparative observations of Captain Pérouse. As for Nordyke's use of John Coulter's comment on Moloka'i's population distribution in 1853, I frankly am puzzled: the area he describes as the center of population *is* the windward side of the island. Nordyke's citation simply supports my argument—and I can only thank her for it while wondering what she thought she was doing in using it. What should be added, however, is that Coulter's observation was made for Moloka'i in the mid-19th century, when the greatly depleted population was concentrated on the *southern* windward side; the archaeological evidence is unambiguous regarding its concentration in pre-*haole* times: as Patrick Kirch puts it, in a summary observation, the "prehistoric Hawaiian population was concentrated on the eastern [windward] part of the island, along the southeast coastline *and* in the four windward valleys." The leeward side, in contrast, was "arid" and "only scantly populated"—as it is today.[3] (Incidentally, as can be seen by comparing this observation with the map of Moloka'i's ancient districts on page 20, Moloka'i provides another example of my contention that population densities were far greater in the smaller—and almost invariably windward—political districts.) There is, simply, no evidence, archaeological or otherwise, to contradict the plain fact that the settlement of the various islands began, quite logically and intelligently, on the wet windward coasts and remained concentrated there even after population pressures forced newer settlements inland and to the dry leeward areas.[4]

The next set of comments by Nordyke and Schmitt concerns the middle section of my essay that discusses pre-*haole* population growth potential, carrying capacity, and the post-*haole* population decline rate.

A) A key issue regarding population growth estimates is the dating of the earliest Hawaiian settlements. In the text I say that the first Polynesians arrived "at least as early as the first century A.D." My supporting citations are to archaeological work that is not yet published, because it is too recent, but that is available upon inquiry. Nordyke's reply is that my statement is wrong, citing for her evidence a textbook discussion that clearly was written and published *before* these new data were available. All I can say to this is that the interested reader is free to do what Nordyke chose not to do: inquire. Or wait for the forthcoming publication of these data. Another forthcoming archaeological assessment draws the same conclusion from these and other even newer studies: "The latest evidence," it is flatly stated, "now suggests that Hawai'i may have been settled as early as the time of Christ."[5] And, I must repeat what I alluded to in the text: the chances of ever finding the earliest site are less than the chances of finding the proverbial needle in a haystack, because this needle almost certainly has a building sitting on top of it. In short, whatever the earliest site discovered (and it is instructive that the "earliest site" dates have been moved back by half a dozen centuries in only the past decade or two of research) it is a virtual certainty that still earlier sites remain permanently buried or destroyed.

B) Nordyke also doubts my hypothesized pre-*haole* population growth rate, noting that correct demographic procedure is to use an S-curve model of growth rather than "geometric progression of an assumed population at an unvarying annual growth rate." Of course, I too note the proper use of a logistic curve to describe long-term population growth (p. 69), but the critical question concerns where on the curve the Hawaiian population was in 1778. We can never know the answer to that question with any precision, but as I demonstrate quite clearly (pp. 66–69) all the historical, anthropological, and paleopathological evidence shows that the population had to have been still expanding at the time of Western contact—that is, it was still ascending and had not yet approached the top of the projected S-curve. Moreover, as Nordyke well knows, in the absence of detailed evidence of historical population growth patterns, it is perfectly conventional for demographic historians to hypothesize a reasonable overall growth rate that is sufficiently modest to take occasional fluctuations and a variety of constraining conditions into consideration—as, for example, Schmitt, Kirch, and others have done with regularity. That is what I did, using a growth rate so conservative that it was designed for a population living under conditions far more severe than those prevailing in pre-*haole* Hawai'i and a population with reproductive rate restrictions that did not obtain in ancient Hawai'i.

C) Both Nordyke and Schmitt express a general intuitive disbelief that the Hawaiian islands could have supported 800,000 people prior to Western contact—despite my pointing out that the resulting population *density* (the critical issue) would have been conventional among eastern Pacific island societies from Easter Island to Tahiti and the Marquesas, and hardly more than moderate for a people living under much harsher conditions with less advanced agricultural and ocean-harvesting knowledge. For example, if Hawai'i in 1778 contained even 600,000 people (at least double the number claimed by Nordyke and Schmitt, but substantially below my estimate) it would have been in the incongruous position of having the lowest population density and by far the richest combination of sea and land resource potential, along with the highest level of agricultural and aquacultural technology, in its part of the world. This, simply, makes no sense. Even tiny, steep, relatively arid, and reefless Nihoa Island to the northeast of Kaua'i once supported a permanent population of such density that if applied to all the Hawaiian islands would push the population well into the millions—as Kenneth Emory demonstrated sixty years ago.[6]

A dubious attitude regarding a large pre-*haole* population for Hawai'i based merely on an impressionistic comparison with today's population not only ignores dramatic differences beween pre-*haole* and present-day population distribution, as I pointed out in the text (p. 43), but when focused on such matters as the alleged "need" for today's population to import food (as Nordyke's comment does) it ignores the fact that only about one in fifty of Hawai'i's people today are in the business of food resource production (and most of that is sugar and pineapple for export), whereas food resource production was the primary task of the vast majority of ancient Hawaiians. This error is a variant (albeit inverted) on what has been called "The Netherlands Fallacy"—the tendency of certain demographers to make facile judgments regarding the over- or under-populated condition of an area without considering the area's particular cultural, environmental, demographic, and social contexts.[7] (Also in this category are Nordyke's rhetorical questions regarding food storage and the absence of "reservoirs"—which is somewhat akin to asking the location of the supermarkets.) Indeed, if Hawai'i's population today *is* about the same size as it was in 1778, it joins the company of a number of areas—including such currently high population growth locales as Peru, central Mexico, Haiti, and the Dominican Republic—that only recently have attained populations as large as those that existed there in the pre-European era.

Schmitt does make two documented comments on this matter, however, that deserve a documented reply. The first of these—that between 36 percent and 50 percent of O'ahu, Maui, and Kaua'i lands have a slope in excess of 20 percent—ignores the well-known fact that sloping land was often intensively farmed in highly productive irrigated terraces by the ancient Hawaiians. (For one example already noted see Figure 3.) Schmitt's observation also fails on the matter of misplaced emphasis: the same data, read with a different eye, show that between one-half and two-thirds of these islands' lands have a slope of *less* than 20 percent—and, as can easily be extrapolated from my earlier carrying capacity discussion in the text, that is 25 to 35 times the land area necessary to support a population of a million people. Moreover, the State of

Hawai'i (Schmitt's source for this information) considers slopes exceeding 35 percent, not 20 percent, too steep for cultivated crops. (See sources in note 8 below.)

As for Schmitt's comments on soil quality, two points need to be made. The first point is very brief: even if we accept at face value Schmitt's use of the state's soil ratings (which, incidentally, take angle of slope into consideration) they show—again, with his emphasis reversed—that 15 percent to 20 percent of the islands' soils (that is, between 600,000 and more than 800,000 acres) are highly hospitable to cultivation. Such acreage is many times what would be necessary to support my hypothesized 1778 population. (See pages 40–41 in the text for discussion of the numbers of people that an acre of cultivated taro land could support.)

That, as I said, is the brief point, accepting Schmitt's use of the state's soil ratings without question. But the fact is that those soil ratings are utterly inappropriate for evaluating pre-1778 agricultural potential because, by giving an inordinate amount of weight to the range of preferred modern crops that a particular area can support, those ratings grossly undervalue land that once was exceptionally productive. As a result, for example, areas with a high water table—areas ideally suited to growing the major Hawaiian subsistence crop of taro—receive the *lowest* possible rating in the state's evaluation scheme. Thus, for instance, Hanalei on Kaua'i, Waipi'o on Hawai'i, and He'eia on O'ahu—all marshy areas famous for their bountiful wetland taro production in both pre- and post-*haole* times—receive in the state's scheme the worst overall productivity rating of "E" (that is, below 30 on the scale of 0 to 100), or, in the official translation of that rating, "very poor suitability for agricultural use."[8] (See Figures 6 and 7.)

The manifest absurdity of using this sort of rating system to estimate pre-*haole* subsistence agricultural potential is made all the more evident by observing that not only are the rich wetlands in the major islands' windward areas thus greatly undervalued, but, in addition, many heavily cultivated leeward areas (such as the huge Kona and Kohala field systems on Hawai'i that so astonished the earliest Westerners with their immense productivity—and that now are known to have been even larger than previously thought, with room left for further expansion)[9] were situated in soils that would have received relatively *low* ratings on Schmitt's scale.

In sum, by introducing into the discussion the state of Hawai'i's

Figure 6. Taro fields in the He'eia wetlands on O'ahu (ca. 1930), an area that receives the State of Hawai'i's lowest rating for agricultural suitability today. (Courtesy of Bishop Museum Photo Archives.)

current land classification system, Schmitt has shown precisely the opposite of what he intended: the islands' soils—magnificently worked by so-called "primitive" agricultural techniques—were capable of furnishing traditional Hawaiian produce yields sufficient to support a population dozens of times larger than what I am proposing in this work.

D) Schmitt and Nordyke also both express doubts about the population decline rate I proposed for the post-1778 era, but only Schmitt produces specific positive evidence in support of his doubt —the "exceptions" of Sāmoa and Tonga to the general pattern of decline in indigenous societies following Western contact. I did not include Sāmoa or Tonga in my list of examples (pp. 46–49) not because they were exceptions that I wished to avoid, but because we know so little about their epidemiological or demographic histories for the years immediately following Western contact. However, what we do know tells a very different story than Schmitt suggests.

Figure 7. The vast rice and taro fields of Hanalei on Kaua'i, another example of the extraordinary fecundity of land that carries the lowest agricultural suitability rating by today's governmental standards. (Courtesy of Bishop Museum Photo Archives.)

Sāmoa. The first real Western contact with Sāmoa occurred in 1768 when Captain Louis Antoine de Bougainville sent a party ashore because of sickness among his crew. The Sāmoans were very unfriendly. Thus, future explorers tended to avoid Sāmoa when possible—and when it proved not possible they received the expected welcome, sometimes worse. But over the decades contacts were made, often between Sāmoans and sick and dying European sailors. The first estimate of Sāmoa's population was not made until 1839, however—seventy-one years after the first European contact. That estimate recorded a population in excess of 56,000 Sāmoans. After that there are copious records of Sāmoans continuing to be assaulted by epidemics of influenza, whooping cough, dysentery, mumps, and other diseases that commonly prove disastrous when introduced to non-immune populations. In 1874, thirty-five years after the first population estimate, a missionary census counted just over 34,000 Sāmoans; five years later a British Consulate estimate reported 31,000.[10] In short, *not considering* the probable population decline between the time of initial contact with diseased Europeans and the first recorded population estimate nearly three-quarters of a century later, the Sāmoan population appears to have declined by about 40 percent to 45 percent in just the thirty-five to forty years between 1839 and 1874–79. That is a holocaust-level decline. And we shall never know what horrors transpired during those earlier seven decades.

Tonga. Again, no contemporary population estimates for the time of first European contact exist, although Captain Abel Tasman reached the islands in 1643 and Captain Cook spent time there in 1773 and again in 1777. During the latter visit Lieutenant King wrote that he could not "make even a tolerable guess" as to the all-island population, but he noted that on any given island "at the time that their entertainments were exhibit'd there might be not short of 12,000 people" in a single place and at one ceremony "we suppose not less than 600 chiefs were assembled." In any case, whatever the total population at the time, contact with the Europeans was already proving catastrophic. As Cook's surgeon, William Anderson, reported in 1777: among the Tongans "the most destructive [disease] is a European one introduc'd amongst them most probably by the ships that visited them in 1773, which has already begun to make fatal ravages amongst them." Anderson was speaking of syphilis and "the misery . . . not only entailed upon thousands who now live but must of necessity be convey'd to endless generations"—and, of course, Anderson himself was spreading his own fatal case of tuberculosis even as he lamented the depredations of syphilis. When the first missionaries arrived twenty years later the Tongans expressed fear that these latest visitors had been sent to bring disease to destroy the natives, a sure indication that the Tongans had suffered greatly from the diseases left by Cook. (Similar expressions of fearful concern greeted missionaries and other Western visitors to Tahiti and Hawai'i after their epidemiological disasters had begun.) The Tongans' fears were well founded: between 1799 and 1826 approximately a quarter of the remaining population was destroyed, in part by one epidemic that "raged so badly," one Westerner reported, "that they were not able to carry the dead away and bury them." Finally, twenty years later (in 1847) missionaries reported the population of Tonga to be "about fifty thousand." By the early 1890s an official census listed the population at just over 19,000—a greater than 60 percent collapse in the half century since the 1847 count, a half century of documented epidemics of terrible "fevers," diarrhea, whooping cough, and much else.[11] More than 60 percent in half a century—and this is not counting the decline between the time of Cook and the missionary arrivals, the 25 percent decline between 1799 and 1826, or the unestimated decline between 1826 and 1847. In sum, again, the dimensions of the overall collapse were staggering.

Now, Schmitt may consider catastrophes such as these "modest declines," to use his phrase. (One can only wonder what he would think of that phrase if he were Sāmoan or Tongan.) But while there is no doubt that many of these early numbers are only rough guesses that either may be too high or too low (which is why I excluded Sāmoa and Tonga from my references in the text), there is no reason for contending that these island groups represent "exceptions" to the examples of population collapse that abounded —and indeed were the norm—throughout the Pacific, the Americas, and elsewhere following the Western invasions.

E) On this same matter of the rate of population decline in Hawai'i, Schmitt attempts to explain the mysterious sudden acceleration of his presumed rate of decline as soon as the missionaries began taking careful censuses. (See my discussion on p. 50.) In response to my contention that this apparent abrupt acceleration did not in fact occur and that actually it is a statistical artifact caused by Schmitt's gross underestimate of the size of the pre-*haole* population and its rapid rate of decline between 1778 and the early 1830s, Schmitt insists that the acceleration did occur, and that it did so as a result of the California gold rush and the shortened voyages of disease-carrying ships to Hawai'i from the mainland United States after 1848. This is an interesting idea that would be more interesting if there were specific data to support it. But even with all the supporting data one could hope for (and ignoring the fact that Schmitt's own tracing of the population decline trajectory, based on census data, correctly shows it slowing rather than accelerating after mid-century—see line A at 75 years on Figure 4, p. 51), it is a supposition with one fatal flaw:

Schmitt's illusory acceleration of the Hawaiian population decline rate first appears around 1830, *not* in the late 1840s and 1850s. In short, Schmitt's explanation is, chronologically, the equivalent to claiming that the stock market collapse of 1929 was caused by the Cold War of the 1950s; alas, the most elementary rules of logic require recognition of the fact that event *A* cannot have caused event *B* if event *A* occured *after* event *B*.

F) Like Schmitt, Nordyke also questions my proposed rate of population decline for the decades immediately following Western contact, in her case contending that if such a decline had occured it would have been mentioned by the early explorers and would have been reflected in the size of burial sites. As to the first of these points, the early explorers who had any basis for comparison (that is, those who visited Hawai'i more than once) in fact *did* comment on the great population collapse, as I will show in a moment. Others, without a basis for comparison, would be no more likely to comment on population decline than were later explorers like Golovnin who, as we have seen, assumed the population to have been unchanged during the previous forty years when even Nordyke admits it declined by 40 to 50 percent. Adding to the "invisibility" of the decline for Westerners only passing through Hawai'i was the fact that so much of the population collapse was attributable not to the physically evident ravages of disease—although, as we saw earlier, those did exist and were commented on[12]—but to high infant mortality and an utterly devastated birth rate. Thus, for example, a median annual birth rate of 19.3 per thousand and a death rate of 47.3—the *actual* figures, calculated by Schmitt, for available locales on O'ahu, Kaua'i, and Hawai'i in the 1830s and early 1840s *when there were no major epidemics*[13]—would have cut the 1778 population more than in half by 1804, exactly as claimed by Malo and in perfect accord with my hypothesized population decline from 800,000 in 1778. [See trajectory of Figure 5 on page 51.] This rate of decline would have left a population of about 380,000 before the terrible *ma'i 'ōku'u* epidemic, setting a pace well ahead of what would have been required to reduce the population at the overall rate I have hypothesized.

For an example of an early explorer who did have a basis for comparison (to expand a bit on the comments in my essay) Captain George Vancouver, who had been with the Cook expedition in 1778–79, returned in the 1790s to find an enormous decline in population, describing "intirely abandoned" villages and areas where population was "reduced at least two-thirds of its size, since the years 1778 and 1779"; he noted, as well, that "places where, on my former visits, the houses were most numerous, was now a clear space, occupied by grass and weeds"—and even the entire island of Lānaʻi, which in 1778-79 Lieutenant King had described as "very pleasant . . . and full of villages," was by 1792 reduced to a "dreary and desolate" place of "apparent sterility" with but a "few scattered miserable habitations."[14]

Although Vancouver admitted that the language barrier made communication with the Hawaiians difficult, he conjectured that the great decline was caused by warfare; others, such as Shaler (cited by Schmitt), later guessed that internal migrations had caused the appearance of population decline. But, as discussed previously, neither of these explanations has weathered historical scrutiny. There were wars, of course, and there were internal migrations, but everything now points (as the Hawaiians had said all along) to disease and a disastrously plummeting birth rate as the primary causes of the great decline. As for the posthumous whereabouts of this once huge population (a question that Nordyke now asks, but that apparently never troubled her when operating under the conventional assumption that the population dropped "only" from about 300,000 to about 140,000 in just four and a half decades) we must recall that we are all writing two centuries after the fact; throughout the 19th century many writers commented on the sand dunes of the islands being littered with skeletons by the "thousands," of beaches "white with human bones" more numerous "than a man would care to count in a day," and of mountain crossings with mounds of "bleached human bones lying at the foot of the precipice."[15] The evidence, in short, was everywhere.

The final set of comments by Schmitt and Nordyke concerns the last section of my essay that discusses possible pre-*haole* diseases, warfare, and other alleged phenomena that, in theory at least, could have slowed the pre-1778 growth rate.

A) Nordyke says she thinks my posited pre-*haole* growth rate (which, as I noted several times, is unrealistically low so as to account for warfare, crop failures, and other catastrophic contingencies) should be reduced further to take account of diseases *possibly* introduced by "occasional migrants," wars brought by "strangers," and other phenomena such as homicide, accidents, inter-district wars, and "lack of modern sanitation." As the reader of this work knows, I have discussed all of these latter concerns and more in the text: even if any of these occasionally raised mortality to uncommon levels (something for which there is in fact no good evidence), nothing in this litany of chimerical population checks is sufficient to reduce my already understated hypothesized growth rate.

As for diseases supposedly introduced by "occasional migrants," again there simply is no evidence that any such thing ever happened with any consequence; and if there is one thing we must do in studying matters as necessarily speculative as this, it is to be guided by the evidence that we do have and not by conjectured "possibilities." Moreover, the only story of "occasional migrants" to Hawai'i during the pre-*haole* era that has even a shred of credibility involves other Polynesians (see note 17 below) whose own post-Western histories of epidemiological disaster indicate they were as free from major infections as were the Hawaiians. Tales of pre-Cook Western "discoveries" of Hawai'i—including an apocryphal Spanish voyage of the mid-16th century—were effectively disposed of by Henry Restarick in 1930.[16] In short, Nordyke's evidentiary ground here is nothing more than her own imagination.

Nordyke does, however, introduce what she considers to be evidence regarding a fancied invasion in the 13th century when (so a single old Hawaiian woman allegedly said seven hundred years later) "tall fierce [Tahitian] warriors" who "did not believe in the force of light" allegedly arrived "in mighty armies that killed, took, and plundered" and caused the sea to "turn red with the blood" of thousands of slaughtered and enslaved Hawaiians. This is a good story. So is the story, reputedly told by the same woman and reported in the same book, *Tales From the Night Rainbow*, that ancient Hawaiians "could do all things" and were not bound by the "laws of life or death"; that they could send their minds great distances "to check out weather conditions, to see a loved one far away, to fly with the birds." And more. The most revealing thing about the appearance of this citation in the guise of serious historical evidence is that Nordyke is reduced to using it in the absence of *any* scholarly support for her belief that such an invasion ever took place or that large numbers of Hawaiians routinely died in ancient warfare.[17] As in all scholarly disciplines, history has rules of evidence; to ignore such rules (or, alternatively, to display unblushingly an unfamiliarity with them) while at the same time claiming to write serious history, is professionally a very perilous act.

In any case, the best study of the consequences of the worst wars ever fought in Hawai'i—wars which occured *after* Western contact—remains the fifty year old work of John F. G. Stokes who showed that in general "battle mortality was slight" and that traditional accounts of battle death (including those repeated by Kamakau and quoted by Nordyke) were greatly inflated. In fact, as I point out in the text (p. 95, note 50), even Schmitt agrees on this point. Despite all the purple prose surrounding tales of military massacres in pre-*haole* Hawai'i, we know as little about the actual consequences of those wars as we do of the skirmishes that occurred elsewhere in the pre-European Pacific.

Indeed, the ferociousness of even the post-European wars in Polynesia has been exaggerated enormously by popular writers. Contemporary observers—explorers and missionaries alike—noted that, when engaged in battle, the Tahitians, for example, "do very little mischief to each other. They seldom come to a serious charge, but content themselves with the execution they are able to effect with slinging stones, by which men are sometimes killed." That writer was William Bligh. Later, missionary James Wilson added that, among the Tahitians, to run away in war, rather than to fight and be wounded or killed, was not at all disgraceful; rather, not to run when in danger was considered foolish. And this was Tahiti *after* European contact when, writes Douglas Oliver, "the presence of European persons and implements began to influence Maohi polity and martial practice." As for earlier times, in Hawai'i as well as Tahiti and elsewhere, in Oliver's words, "there has come down to us little information save ambiguous legends and biased chronicle"—but there is certainly no reason to believe that pre-*haole* warfare was any more murderous than its relatively mild post-*haole* version.[18]

B) The only other alleged check on pre-*haole* population growth that receives even the appearance of evidentiary support is that old chestnut, infanticide. Against the wealth of solid evidence that I produce in the text—both historical and scientific—showing that infanticide was not a common, culturally approved practice in pre-*haole* Hawai'i (pp. 63–65), Nordyke quotes the one source invariably used by those who bother to cite anyone when claiming that infanticide was rampant in those times—a missionary-edited and translated newspaper article written in 1867 by a Christianized and evangelical Hawaiian chronicler, Samuel M. Kamakau. However, not only is this tainted and secondary source material—and not only is the translation willfully misrendered, with, for example, no mention made in the original Hawaiian text of *kahuna 'o'o* or of the present tense, and with at least one instance of the word for "abortion" mistranslated as "infanticide"—the crucial point is that, as is shown by the very words Nordyke has chosen to quote, Kamakau was referring to Hawai'i "in pagan days," which means before the arrival of the missionaries in 1820.[19] That was 42 years after the first Europeans had introduced syphilis and gonorrhea with their devastating impact on fertility, stillbirth, infant mortality, and gross congenital malformation. Although to this day there is no good evidence of a high rate of infanticide even during those 42 years of post-*haole* "pagan days," it is at least possible that in such an environment infanticide would occur with increased frequency *or* that the high rate of infant loss would be misinterpreted by non-Hawaiian speaking early missionaries as evidence of such anticipated "savage" traits as infanticide. (The first serious discussion of infanticide as an alleged practice comes from the pen of missionary William Ellis, just arrived in Hawai'i from Tahiti where at least one segment of the population probably did practice infanticide at a rate perhaps as high as was common in 18th century England or France.) But, as noted earlier, *all* the evidence, without exception, regarding the pre-1778 period in Hawai'i—from the first-hand observations of independent Western visitors at different times to modern scientific analyses of skeletal remains—points *only* in the direction of an extremely low infant mortality rate from all causes and directly contradicts the notion of a significant level of infanticide. The mere repetition of missionary-inspired fables is insufficient argument in the face of a wealth of genuine scholarly data.

C) Lastly, on the matter of the exceptional health of the Hawaiians prior to Western contact, Schmitt raises two objections: first, he confidently asserts, the ancient Hawaiians were indeed afflicted with epidemic diseases; second, he notes, their life expectancy was no more than 30 years. These require some discussion; I will take them one at a time.

Epidemics. Against all the overwhelming evidence that has accumulated during decades of scientific study showing the virtual absence of major infectious diseases among ancient Hawaiians, Schmitt claims that such diseases *did* exist and for evidence he introduces a citation from the 19th century Hawaiian writer David Malo that "recalled two exceptionally destructive epidemics, the *mai ahulau* in Waia's reign and *hai-lepo* at a later date." What Schmitt fails to do here, however, is to inquire as to *who* this Waia fellow was or when he "reigned." A little investigation would have revealed that this bit of datum has about as much serious historical credibility as does Nordyke's quotation from *Tales From the Night Rainbow*—which is to say, none. Waia, Schmitt should have known, was the *legendary* son of Haloa in one version of Hawaiian mythology and the grandchild of Papa and Wakea—the spiritual Earth Mother and Sky Father—who, in the traditional Hawaiian creation myth, brought forth the Hawaiian islands. In this myth Waia is portrayed as a corrupt and evil ruler whose reign was despoiled by a plague that left precisely twenty-six persons alive. (The other legendary epidemic, *hai-lepo,* supposedly left exactly sixteen people alive.) To use patent mythology of this sort as historical authentication for the claimed actual occurrence of mundane past events is equivalent to alleging that fratricide was common in the ancient Near East and introducing as the *sole* piece of evidence the Biblical myth that Cain slew Abel. This is, to put it gently, grasping at straws. Beyond that, it says something important about selective use of data when Schmitt employs this sort of fictitious story from Malo as "evidence" while ignoring directly contradictory statements by Kamakau and, in other places, rejecting out of hand Malo's *first hand* description of the great population collapse that in fact *did* occur during Malo's own lifetime.[20]

Life expectancy. Again, this is a subject briefly dealt with in the text (page 91, note 20), but that apparently requires some expansion. (I must note at the outset, however, that my proposed pre-*haole* population growth rate is so conservative that among its particulars it *assumes* an unrealistically low life expectancy of about age thirty—the same age cited by Schmitt—and thus it is untouched by Schmitt's point here.) It has been known for many years that the weakest aspect of paleodemographic analysis is the computation of life expectancy or the average age at death of ancient peoples. Individuals from different ethnic and racial groups in different environmental settings manifest different skeletal changes at different ages. Thus, without a demographic model drawn from actual study of the living population in question—comparing empirically *known* age at death with *observed* skeletal changes in the construction of the model—all such historical age estimates are guesses that paradoxically assume the major part of what is attempting to be studied, a paradox necessitated by the fact that there are by definition no living individuals from whom to construct an empirical model or life-table. To avoid complete tautology in such research, models are constructed from what are hoped may be fairly comparable populations. In the case of ancient Hawaiians the "comparable" populations generally used are modern North American Plains Indians—a major stretch of the imagination, to say the least.

Moreover, compounding this difficulty is the fact that such studies admittedly (in the words of one of the reigning experts in the field) "have one apparently chronic problem in that they seem systematically to under-age adults."[21] This is because, among other things, skeletons of people estimated to have lived to age fifty and beyond are lumped into a single category. Skeletal distinctions of persons beyond age fifty are so minor as to force this procedure, but the consequence is that any population containing people older than fifty is systematically under-aged. Thus, for example, assuming everything else were perfect, a future paleodemographic study of the American population today, using these same techniques, would report a life expectancy somewhere in the mid-to late forties—almost thirty years too short!

Now, because of the known exceptional longevity of Americans today, no doubt this is an extreme case. But common sense works the other way as well. The same study that Schmitt cites as identifying the pre-*haole* Hawaiian life expectancy as less than thirty years (a study co-authored by Schmitt) reports a life expectancy of thirty-five to thirty-six years among Hawaiians living on northern

Kaua'i in 1847—that is, 20 percent *higher* than the alleged pre-1778 life expectancy. Yet, by 1847 the people of northern Kaua'i (like their brethren throughout the islands) were wracked by syphilis, gonorrhea, tuberculosis, and other fatal diseases they had not had prior to 1778 and were dying off in such large numbers that year after year the mission station reports listed deaths as exceeding births by ratios of 2, 3, and 4 to 1—and in some epidemic years it was even worse. So bad was the situation at this time that missionaries stationed in the very districts to which Schmitt refers constantly wrote of "death making its ravages among the people," endlessly reminding them that their "days [are] like a shadow" and warning that if the present rate of decline persists there will soon be no more Hawaiians at all, "for they are rapidly melting away."[22] Although Schmitt's cited calculation of a life expectancy rate for this population of thirty-five or thirty-six years appears correct, it is flatly nonsensical to think that a people in this diseased and devastated condition, with a fertility rate so low they seem to observers on the way to extinction, would produce an average life expectancy 20 percent *higher* than that of the robust population, with healthy children everywhere, that Cook and his crews encountered in 1778-79. The case of Hawai'i, if anything, underlines the understated 1985 assertion by a *defender* of the beleaguered field of paleodemography that, in light of "recent and sometimes scathing criticisms," certain reconsiderations of the field "require immediate attention. Particularly crucial is the need to refine methods for accurately estimating age in older adults and to standardize aging techniques across observers."[23] In sum, although an average Hawaiian life expectancy of only thirty years in the pre-*haole* era would not affect my proposed average population growth rate one bit, there is little doubt that an accurate assessment would peg that life expectancy rate (and, consequently, the growth rate) significantly higher.

Of course, I must acknowledge that the use and citation of modern scholarly work such as this invites Schmitt's criticism that it represents, in his words, "trendiness and the scholarly bandwagon." More than anything, however, this rejoinder reveals in Schmitt an attitude that only can be greeted with sadness—particularly since the specific target of his comment (the allegedly "trendy" research and analysis of Borah and Cook) began half a century ago and has represented conventional scholarly opinion for more than two decades.

This completes my reply to the comments by Nordyke and Schmitt. It hardly, however, completes the debate. In her opening remarks Nordyke contends that "the final answer" as to the question of Hawai'i's pre-*haole* population size invariably must be a confession of "futility." "The true number is ultimately unknowable," adds Schmitt—noting in a personal communication to me that "the longer I ponder this problem the more skeptical I become of *all* precensal estimates, including my own."

Perhaps. But Nordyke will continue to issue new editions of her book, *The Peopling of Hawai'i*, and Schmitt will continue to contribute to new editions of *The Atlas of Hawai'i*—both of them containing estimates of the pre-*haole* population—while scholars studying other aspects of Hawai'i's past will require as good an estimate of the 1778 population as is available. What numbers will they use? And how will they justify their selection? Nordyke and Schmitt, having challenged my new estimate (unsuccessfully, I think it is clear), apparently remain content with the conventional figures of 200,000 to 300,000. As I said at the beginning of my study, however, that conventional estimate today is based *entirely* on Schmitt's unsystematic critique of Lieutenant King's 18th century calculations, nothing more; and it is a critique, we have seen, that not only is unsystematic, but that is riddled with such flagrant errors of fact and judgment that, once exposed, they leave the resulting estimate with no credibility whatsoever—other than what is derived from the mere habit of friendly repetition.

In justifying their continued support for the conventional estimate, then, Schmitt, Nordyke, and other like-minded scholars have two clear intellectual and professional responsibilities: first, as I said in closing the body of my essay, if the population was less than 800,000 "it is now incumbent on those who would hold this position to demonstrate—*in specific scholarly detail*—precisely how it came to be less than what all the evidence suggests is a minimum"; second, it is incumbent on them to advance an equally rigorous and detailed argument *in support* of the 200,000 to 300,000 estimate. If the traditional estimate is to be taken seriously it must be founded on a good deal more than a mistake-filled critique of

King or an equally error-filled collection of quibbles over, at most, peripheral points in my estimate. Mere appeals to past "authority" will no longer do, either. Nor will the empty repetition of now demonstrably discredited canards such as the alleged pre-1778 pandemics of infanticide, warfare, human sacrifice, and the like— or the straightforward misuse of mythology and legend as a substitute for historical data.

These are serious matters. They require serious study. It makes an enormous difference to the work of anthropologists and archaeologists, as well as to cultural, intellectual, social, and political historians—to say nothing of the Hawaiian people today— whether there were a quarter of a million Hawaiians in 1778 or three-quarters of a million. Or more. Indeed, once the reality of these larger numbers is admitted, major revisions will be required in every aspect of both pre- and post-*haole* Hawaiian history.

For there is no point in denying that this is a subject with powerful social and political ramifications. A people, after all, are what their historical experience—and their knowledge of it— has made them, which is why governments often have a meddlesome interest in the history that is written during their watch. To native peoples, who have suffered so terribly and in so many ways as the victims of every sort of Western cultural avarice, knowledge of the size of their populations prior to Western contact is a matter of crucial historical importance. It is equally important, for opposite reasons, to the Westerners who caused the suffering. This is not only because large populations conventionally imply sophisticated systems of governance and resource distribution (something which colonizers, in their efforts to justify conquest as beneficial to the conquered, would prefer the colonized not know about their pasts), but also because the larger the population on the eve of Western contact, the greater the subsequent horror. For those who bring on a holocaust, willfully or not, nothing is more desirable or sought after than historical amnesia. Thus, the politics of this subject. And thus, the assurance that debate has just begun.

NOTES

1. Because it would distract attention away from the specific population issues at hand, I have chosen not to discuss in the main body of my reply Nordyke's displeasure with my use of the phrase "pre-*haole*" as a shorthand for the period of

Hawaiian history prior to 1778. A brief note, however, seems in order. I decided to use the word *haole* in this context for two reasons: first, as a synonym for "pre-Caucasian" or "pre-European," "pre-*haole*" is more precise than "pre-contact" which is ambiguous unless laden with the conventional arrogance of assuming that the only culture "contacts" that matter in the histories of indigenous peoples are their contacts with white people; second, *haole* is a widely-understood Hawaiian word that even 19th century missionaries used in referring to themselves, and it seems both appropriate and preferable, when in Hawai'i and writing about Hawaiian history, to use Hawaiian phrases when they do not hinder communication with English-only speakers. (Schmitt, it is worth noting, does something similar by closing his comment with the remark that he "must still vote *kānalua*"; in the Territorial Legislature it was the practice to abstain from a vote by saying *"kānalua"*—though I have the distinct impression that Schmitt is not abstaining here.) In finding "a negative racial overtone" in my choosing to employ the phrase "pre-*haole*," Nordyke expresses more than anything else a strikingly defensive hypersensitivity. This is all the more noteworthy in view of her (and Schmitt's) frequent use of the word "primitive" to describe Hawaiians and her expressed preference for "pre-historic" and (in her book, *The Peopling of Hawai'i*) "stone age" as terms to describe Hawai'i prior to the arrival of *haoles*. "Pre-history," of course, is a term invented in imperialistic 19th century Britain to distinguish between the pasts of literate and non-literate peoples. Not only is it a "simple-minded" term—to use the apt phrase of Cambridge anthropologist Jack Goody—but (like the offhand use of the terms "stone age" and "primitive"), the most revealing aspect of the belief that "history" for most indigenous peoples only begins when they are intruded upon by whites is the accompanying implicit message of white cultural and racial supremacy. [The Goody reference is from his book, *The Domestication of the Savage Mind* (Cambridge: Cambridge University Press, 1977), p. 14.]

2. On Kona see C. T. Kawachi, "Radiocarbon Dates From an Upland Site of the Kona Field System, Hawai'i Island, Hawai'i," *Radiocarbon*, 28 (1986), 1227. On Waimea see Jeffrey T. Clark, "Waimea-Kawaihae, a Leeward Hawai'i Settlement System" (Doctoral Dissertation: University of Illinois, 1987). On the example of Mākaha see Roger C. Green, *Mākaha Before 1880 A.D.* (Honolulu: Bishop Museum Pacific Archaeological Records-31, 1980).

3. Patrick Kirch, *Feathered Gods and Fishhooks* (Honolulu: University of Hawai'i Press, 1985), pp. 123-24, emphasis added.

4. See the concise discussion of this in Green, *Mākaha Before 1880*, pp. 71-72.

5. Matthew Spriggs and Malcolm Chun, "Renaming the Hawaiian Cultural Sequence," in P. B. Griffin and M. Spriggs, eds., *New Directions in Hawaiian Archaeology: Papers in Honor of Kenneth Emory*, forthcoming.

6. Kenneth P. Emory, *Archaeology of Nihoa and Necker Islands* (Honolulu: Bishop Museum Press, 1928).

7. Paul R. Ehrlich and John P. Holdren, "Impact of Population Growth," *Science*, 171 (1971), 1214. Nordyke herself, incidentally, estimates an equal or higher population in pre-*haole* times than today for every island except O'ahu.

8. The detailed area ratings and operational definitions can be found in the

Land Study Bureau's *Detailed Land Classification* volumes for the individual islands (Honolulu: University of Hawai'i Press, 1972), volumes 2 (Kaua'i), 6 (Hawai'i), and 11 (O'ahu).

9. On the Kona and Kohala field systems, see Matthew Spriggs, "Adornment or Degradation? Prehistoric Human Impact on the Hawaiian Landscape," in Griffin and Spriggs, eds., *New Directions in Hawaiian Archaeology*.

10. Charles Wilkes, *Narrative of the United States Exploring Expedition During the Years 1838, 1839, 1840, 1841, 1842* (London: Wiley & Putnam, 1845), Volume II, p. 130; various estimates in the same general range for the 1870s are reported most conveniently (though with typically partisan commentary) in Norma McArthur, *Island Populations of the Pacific* (Canberra: Australian National University Press, 1968), pp. 107–108. Peter Pirie takes particular aim at McArthur's mistreatment of the data on Sāmoa in his review of her work in *Australian Geographical Studies*, 6 (1968), esp. 176–78.

11. James King, "Journal," in J. C. Beaglehole, ed., *The Journals of Captain James Cook* (Cambridge: Hakluyt Society and the University Press, 1967), Volume III, Part Two, pp. 1364–65; William Anderson, "Journal," in ibid., p. 927; McArthur, *Island Populations*, pp. 71–76.

12. In addition to previously cited sources on this, note that *every* extant journal of the men aboard the Russian vessels *Nadezhda* and *Neva*, which visited Hawai'i in 1804, commented on the horrible effects of syphilis evident on the bodies of almost all the Hawaiians they encountered. And they avoided visiting O'ahu because of the *ma'i 'ōku'u* that was raging at the time. The most convenient collection of these journals is Glynn Barratt, *The Russian Discovery of Hawai'i: The Journals of Eight Russian Explorers* (Honolulu: Editions Limited, 1987).

13. Robert C. Schmitt, *The Missionary Censuses of Hawai'i* (Honolulu: Bishop Museum Press, 1973), p. 13.

14. George Vancouver, *A Voyage of Discovery . . . Round the World* (London, 1798), Volume I, pp 158–60, 187–88.

15. John F. G. Stokes, "Dune Sepulture, Battle Mortality, and Kamehameha's Alleged Defeat on Kaua'i," *Hawaiian Historical Society Report*, 45 (1936), 36; Samuel M. Kamakau, *Ruling Chiefs of Hawai'i* (Honolulu: Kamehameha Schools Press, 1961), p. 235; L. Vernon Briggs, *Experience of a Medical Student in Honolulu in 1881* (Boston: Nickerson, 1926), p. 31.

16. Henry B. Restarick, *The Discovery of Hawai'i* (Honolulu: Hawaiian Historical Society, 1930).

17. Pali Lee and Koko Willis, *Tales From the Night Rainbow* (Honolulu: privately printed, 1987), p. 59. This fictitious tale of the great Tahitian invasion is an enormously exaggerated version of a traditional Hawaiian story about a small 12th century migration from Tahiti—and a subsequent period of two-way voyaging between Hawai'i and Tahiti. Even this more modest rendition, however, has long been doubted by most scholars. See, for example, R. H. Cordy, "The Tahitian Migration to Hawai'i ca. 1100–1300 A.D.: An Argument Against its Occurrence," *New Zealand Archaeological Association Newsletter*, 17 (1974), 65–76 and R. C. Green, "Tahiti-Hawai'i, A.D. 1100–1300: Further Comments," *New Zealand Archaeological Association Newsletter*, 17 (1974), 206–12. The evidence

that does exist suggests, at most, that "a few voyaging canoes may have arrived in Hawai'i from central East Polynesia" during this period; and "[w]hile the new arrivals might have been well received, and even accorded the status of chiefs . . . their influence on the course of Hawaiian cultural development was unlikely to have been great." (Kirch, *Feathered Gods and Fishhooks*, p. 305.) Of course, this—the commonly accepted scholarly opinion—might be wrong. A forthcoming essay by Matthew Spriggs, "The Hawaiian Transformation of Ancestral Polynesian Society: Conceptualizing Chiefly States," contends, for example, that a very small number of Tahitian immigrants could have had a significant impact on Hawaiian religious and political ideology, albeit in an indirect fashion. But this sort of subtle and careful scholarship is a far, far cry from *Tales From the Night Rainbow*. (The matter of warfare is discussed below.)

18. Stokes, "Dune Sepulture," passim; Ida Lee, *Captain Bligh's Second Voyage to the South Sea* (London: Longmans, Green, 1920), pp. 73–74; James Wilson, *A Missionary Voyage to the Southern Pacific Ocean, Performed in the Years 1796, 1797, 1798* (London: T. Chapman, 1799), p. 363; Douglas L. Oliver, *Ancient Tahitian Society* (Honolulu: University of Hawai'i Press, 1974), Volume I, p. 388. In addition, some of the other early Western observations suggest that Tahitian warfare—like Hawaiian—may well have been more ritualistic than murderous. The best source here is probably José Andia y Varela, *Relacion d'un voyage a l'ile d'amat ou Taiti . . . en 1774* (Paris, 1835), portions of which are translated in Bolton Glanville Corney, ed., *The Quest and Occupation of Tahiti . . .* (London: Cambridge University Press, 1915), Volume Two. Similar conditions existed throughout the Pacific. For another example of a supposedly warlike society in which very few people were ever killed in battle, see Ron Adams's discussion of the case of Vanuatu (formerly the New Hebrides) in *In the Land of Strangers: A Century of European Contact with Tanna* (Canberra: Australian National University Press, 1984), p. 12. Finally, it is worth noting that pre-European contact warfare among native peoples—not only in the Pacific, but throughout the world—was commonly less destructive than is popularly supposed. For a good recent analysis of some North American Indian societies in this regard, see Adam J. Hirsch, "The Collision of Military Cultures in Seventeenth-Century New England," *Journal of American History*, 74 (1988), 1187–1212.

19. I am grateful to Professor Lilikalā Kame'eleihiwa of the Center for Hawaiian Studies at the University of Hawai'i at Manoa for translating this passage for me.

20. Samuel M. Kamakau, *Ka Po'e Kahiko* (Honolulu: Bishop Museum Press, 1964), p. 109; Schmitt, "The 'Ōku'u."

21. Kenneth M. Weiss, *Demographic Models for Anthropology* (Society for American Archaeology Memoir Number 27—1973), p. 59.

22. Such comments are everywhere in the mission station reports from all the islands during this time; the quoted comments were taken from the Wai'oli (Kaua'i) Station Reports of 1835, 1836, and 1840, on file at the Hawaiian Mission Children's Society Library in Honolulu.

23. Jane E. Buikstra and Lyle W. Konigsberg, "Paleodemography: Critiques and Controversies," *American Anthropologist*, 87 (1985), 330.

INDEX

abortion, 60, 63, 79
Adams, Romanzo, 106, 115
Anahulu (O'ahu), 123
Anderson, Rufus, 66
Anderson, William, 132
Australia, 48

Bangladesh, 33
Bartlett, Samuel, 63
Bayly, William, 5-6, 8-9
Bligh, William, 4, 6, 8, 9, 25, 137
Bliss, Isaac, 56
Borah, Woodrow, xvii, 119, 141
Bougainville, Louis Antoine de, 131
Brazil, 47
Britain, 41-42, 62, 67
bronchiectasis, 71
bronchitis, 70
bubonic plague, 36, 41-42, 55
Buck, Peter (Rangihiroa, Te), 115, 123
Bushnell, Oswald A., 60, 119

California Indians, 47
Campbell, Archibald, 60
carrying capacity, 37-45, 52-53, 79, 112, 116, 127-130
cholera, 55, 112
Cleghorn, Paul L., 78
Clerke, Charles, 15, 70, 71
Cook, James, 3, 9, 50, 59, 70, 79, 106-107, 123-24, 132
Cook, Noble David, 46
Cook, Sherburne, vii, 119, 141
Cook Islands, 48
Crosby, Alfred, 72
Coulter, John W., 109, 125

death/birth ratios, 52, 134, 141
Denison, David, 26
depopulation, 45-52, 53-58, 66-69, 79, 111-12, 115, 117-18, 130-35

Dixon, George, 4-8, 112
Dobyns, Henry, xvii, 6, 22, 75
Dubos, René and Jean, 70-71
Dominican Republic, 128
dysentery, 36, 131

Ellis, William (member Cook's crew), 18, 69, 74
Ellis, William (missionary), 53, 138
Emory, Kenneth, 5, 10-11, 115
'Ewa (O'ahu), 20, 24

fertility, 65-66, 72-73
Florida, 22, 47
Forman, Arthur, 26
Fornander, Abraham, 107, 123

Gilbert, George, 15, 19
Golovnin, V. M., 5-8, 134
gonorrhea, 69, 72-73, 138, 141
Green, J. S., 53
Guatemala, 47

Haiti, 128
Hālawa (Moloka'i), 37
Hālawa (O'ahu), 123
Haleakala (Maui), 24, 37
Hāmākua (Hawai'i), 18-20, 22, 117
Hāna (Maui), 17
Hanalei (Kaua'i), 53, 129, 131
Hassan, Fekri A., 36, 65-66
Hawai'i Island, 4, 10, 12-30, 37, 53-54, 56-57, 69, 71, 117
health, Hawaiian, 60-61, 67-68, 73-78, 119, 138-41
Heddington, Thomas, 26
He'eia (O'ahu) 57, 129, 130
Hilo (Hawai'i), 17, 22, 117
Hispaniola, 40, 46
Hitchcock, H. R., 53
Hommon, Robert J., 19, 36, 66-67, 69

Honokāne (Hawai'i), 18
Honolulu (O'ahu), 56
Hormann, Bernhard, 106, 115
Howe, K. R., xvi

Iceland, 47
infanticide, 60, 63–65, 68, 79, 111, 138, 143
influenza, 62, 70–71, 74–75, 131
Iran, 33
Ireland (potato blight), 36, 67

Japan, 62, 67
Jarves, James Jackson, 54–55
Jennings, Francis, xvii
Johnson, Lent C., 77, 78

Ka'ena Point (Lāna'i), 11
Kahana (O'ahu), 18
Kaho'olawe, 10, 13, 56, 117
Kailua (Hawai'i), 16
Kailua (O'ahu), 57
Kalealoa (O'ahu), 24
Kamakau, Samuel M., 55, 106, 111, 137, 138, 139
Kamehameha I, 16
Kapāpala (Hawai'i), 26
Ka'ū (Hawai'i), 20, 24, 26, 123
Kaua'i, 4, 8, 12–13, 15, 22–23, 29, 37, 43, 56, 69, 70, 71, 107, 117, 123–24, 141
Kaunolū (Lāna'i), 11
Kealakekua Bay, 3, 13–17, 20, 28–30
Ke'anae (Maui), 23
Kelly, Marion, 20
Kenya, 33
Kerley, Ellis R., 77, 78
Keōpū, 76–78
Kīlauea (Kaua'i), 17
King, Ambrose, 77
King, James, 3, 9, 13–31, 46, 50, 57, 59, 60, 64, 69, 78–79, 106, 107, 123–24, 125, 132, 135
Kīpahulu (Maui), 23
Kirch, Patrick Vinton, 33, 63–64, 66–67, 78, 110, 115, 125, 127
Kohala (Hawai'i), 16, 22, 129
Kona (Hawai'i), 20, 123–24, 129
Kona (Kaua'i), 20, 22
Kona (Moloka'i), 20
Ko'olauloa (O'ahu), 43
Kualoa (O'ahu), 43
Kula (Maui), 20

Lahaina, 17, 56
Lāna'i, 4, 10–12, 29, 56, 71, 117, 135
Law, John, 14
Ledyard, John, 15, 28

Lee, Pali, 110
leeward/windward population differential, 17–23, 107–09, 125–26
Lehua, 4, 9–10, 12
leprosy (Hansen's Disease), 112
life expectancy, Hawaiian, 61, 119, 139–41
Līhu'e (Kaua'i), 43
Lind, Andrew, 106, 115
Loomis, Elisha, 15
Luluku (O'ahu), 30, 123

McArthur, Norma, xvi, 34–36, 115–16
McCoid, Catherine Hodge, 25
ma'i 'ōku'u, 55–57, 134
Mākaha (O'ahu), 18, 43, 124
Makahiki, 68
Makawao (Maui), 53
Malo, David, 57–58, 119, 139
Mandan Indians, 49
Mangarevas, 42, 48
Marquesas, 13, 42, 48, 127
Maui, 4, 10, 11, 29, 37, 55–56, 69, 71, 73, 117
measles, 70, 71, 112
Menzies, Archibald, 5–6, 8
Mexico, 47–48, 61, 128
Mohawk Indians, 49
Mōkapu, 76–78, 119
Moloka'i, 4, 12–13, 23, 53, 56, 71, 105, 109, 112, 117, 125–26
mumps, 131

Nā Pali (Kaua'i), 43–44
"Netherlands Fallacy," 128
New Caledonia, xvi, 49
New England Indians, 47
New Guinea, 39
Newman, T. Stell, 20
New Zealand (Aotearoa), 26, 65
Nicaragua, 47
Nicol, Claude, 77
Nigeria, 33
Nihoa, 127
Ni'ihau, 4, 8–10, 12, 56–57, 69, 106, 117, 123–24
Nordyke, Eleanor C., 59–60, 123–43

O'ahu, 4, 12, 23, 29, 37, 43, 55–56, 71, 117
Ojibwa Indians, 49
Oliver, Douglas, 137
osteoperiostitis, 76

Pakistan, 33
Pérouse, J. F. G. de la, 23, 125
Peru, 38–39, 46, 128
Petersen, William, 5

INDEX

Pirie, Peter, 75–76
Pitcairn Island, 33
Pohnpei, 49
Pololū (Hawai'i), 18
population: of the pre-Columbian Americas, xv; of Hawaii, previous estimates, xvi–xvii, 4–5, 59, 78–80, 114, 142; growth rates, 33–37, 62, 65–66, 109–10, 126–27; densities, 38–45, 116–117, 127–28; decline, see depopulation
Portlock, Nathaniel, 9, 71, 112
Puakō (Hawai'i), 17
Pukui, Mary Kawena, 64
Puna (Hawai'i), 18, 22

Rapanui (Easter Island), 42, 48, 127
Restarick, Henry, 136
rickets, 73–74
Rickman, John, 16, 19
"Romer's Rule," 25

sacrifice, human, 60–61, 143
Sahlins, Marshall, 68
Sāmoa, 13, 117, 130–32, 133
Samwell, David, 13, 15, 18–19, 28, 63
Saskatchewan (Canada), 47
Saunders, I. W., 34–36
Schmitt, Robert C., 4–14, 31, 34, 36, 46, 50, 106, 111, 123–43
settlement of Hawai'i, earliest, 32–33, 109–110, 126
smallpox, 36, 70, 112
Snow, Charles, 78
soil productivity, 117, 129–30
Southeast Asia, 62, 67
Starna, William A., 49
Stewart, C. S., 54–55
Stokes, John, 105, 137
Summers, Catherine, 112

Sutton, Douglas G., 65
syphilis, 7, 69–77, 132, 138, 141

Taeuber, Irene, 119
Tahiti, 13, 42, 48, 60, 70, 91–93n.21, 111, 127, 136, 137, 138
Tapituea (Drummond's Island), 40
Tasman, Abel, 132
"thrifty genotype hypothesis," 72
Tonga, 13, 117, 130, 132–33
topography of Hawaiian Islands, 117, 128–29
tuberculosis, 7, 70–73, 77–78, 112, 132, 141
Turnbull, John, 63–64
Tweedie, R. L., 34–36
typhoid fever, 55, 70
typhus, 36, 70

Vancouver, George, 5–6, 10, 112, 134–35
Vanuatu, 48
venereal disease, see syphilis, gonorrhea, and yaws

Waiāhole (O'ahu), 57
Waialua (O'ahu), 43
Wailuku (Maui), 53
Waimea (Hawai'i), 123–24
Waimea (Kaua'i), 6–7, 13, 17–18
Waipi'o (Hawai'i), 18, 129
warfare, 60–62, 111, 136–37, 143
Watt, James, 77
whooping cough, 70, 112, 131, 133
Willis, Koko, 110
Wilson, James, 137
Wohlers, J. F. H., 66
Wyllie, R. C., 52

Yaws, 75–77
Yucatan, 39–40

ABOUT THE AUTHOR

David E. Stannard is Professor of American Studies at the University of Hawai'i. A recipient of numerous grants and awards, including Guggenheim and American Council of Learned Societies research fellowships and a University of Hawai'i Regents' Medal for teaching excellence, his previous books include the widely acclaimed *Shrinking History: On Freud and the Failure of Psychohistory; The Puritan Way of Death: A Study in Religion, Culture, and Social Change;* and an edited collection of essays, *Death in America.* He received his doctorate from Yale University, where he taught in the American Studies and history departments until moving to Hawai'i in 1979.